NINJUTSU
Enduring Legacy

By
James Clum, Shidoshi

The techniques in this book are being demonstrated for educational purposes only. Before beginning any kind of martial arts program or physical exercise, seek the approval of one's physician. The author assumes no responsibility for use or misuse of the information contained within this book resulting in any and all types of injury. Martial arts are inherently dangerous and one could sustain both minor and serious injuries from their practice. Find a qualified instructor.

© 2010 Dr. James Clum
2nd Edition
ISBN 978-0-557-28549-5

Table of Contents

Introduction
    Historical Ninjutsu/7
    Ninjutsu Today/10
    Gyokko Ryu/11
    Gyokko Ryu Lineage Chart/13
A Foundation for Movement
    Yoko Aruki/18
    Ichimonji no Kamae/21
    Jumonji no Kamae/23
    Hicho no Kamae/24
    Shizen no Kamae/25
    Shoshin no Kamae/26
    Hira no Kamae/27
    Suggesting for Practicing Kamae/28
    Additional Kamae/33
    Kihon Sabaki Gata/34
Ukemi Gata Taihenjutsu (Breakfalls, Rolling and Leaping)
    Zenpo Kaiten/40
    Naname Zenpo Kaiten/ 43
    Sayu Kaiten or Yoko Gaeri/46
    Oten/49
    Koho Kaiten and Ushiro Gaeshi/51
    Zenpo Ukemi/53
    Yoko Nagare Ukemi/55
    Koho Ukemi/57
    Shiho Tenchi Tobi/58
    Zenpo Tobi/60
Dakentaijutsu (The Art of Striking)
    Tsuki/64
    Jodan Uke/Nagashi/65
    Gedan Uke/Nagashi/67
Sanshin no Kata (The Three Hearts Forms)
    Chi no Kata/72
    Sui no Kata/75
    Ka no Kata/78
    Fu no Kata/81
    Ku no Kata/84
    Alternative Views/87
Kosshi Sanpo (The Three Methods of Striking Tissues)
    Ichimonji no Kamae/94
    Hicho no Kamae/97
    Jumonji no Kamae/100

Torite Kihon Gohov (The Five Methods of Defending Against Being Seized)
    Omote Gyaku/103
    Omote Gyaku Men Tsuki/106
    Ura Gyaku/108
    Muso Dori/114
    Musha Dori/117
    Ganseki Nage/120
    Oni Kudaki/127
    Take Ori/132
    Hon Gyaku/134
    Taihenjutsu Mutodori Gata/136

Hiken Juruppo (The Sixteen Secret Fists)
    The Sixteen Fists/ 137

Hajutsu Kuho (The Nine Methods of Overpowering)
    Tehodoki/147
    Taihodoki/153
    Oyagoroshi/Kogoroshi/158
    Koshi Kudaki/162
    Keri Kudaki/163
    Ken Kudaki/165
    Toki Kudaki/165
    Happo Keri/166

Putting the Basics Together
    Distance, Timing and Angles/168
    Destroying Form/170
    Simplicity/172
    Connecting Movements/176
    Keep Moving and Wrap Up the Opponent/178
    Changing Against Resistanc/181
    Making Techniques Seemless/183

Togakure Ryu Ninpo Taijutsu
    History/189
    Kamae/191
    Taijutsu Ukemi Gata/196
    Shinobi Gaeshi Gata/213
    Hiden no Gata/215
    Santo Tonko no Gata/217
    Goton no Jutsu/234
    Suiton no Jutsu/237
    Kinton no Jutsu/240
    Mokuton no Jutsu/243
    Doton no Jutsu/245
    Katon no Jutsu/248
    Glossary/252

Preface

Taijutsu is the art or skill of moving the body. A ballet dancer's *taijutsu* is different from a football player's *taijutsu* and so to a large degree our *taijutsu* or body movements are determined by what activities we do. When learning the foundation (*kihon*) of *Budo Taijutsu*, students begin with postures (*kamae*) which reflect a certain attitude, strategy, or feeling. They are photographed as still pictures but really only represent movements in passing time.

Taihenjutsu is the art or skill of "changing the body." Perhaps a smoother way to say this would be "physical adaptation." *Taijutsu* (physical skill) arises from one's ability to improve at an activity and do it more efficiently or skillfully. It does not necessarily imply that one would necessarily be skillful at a similar discipline. For instance, a champion rugby player's skills may not translate into exceptional soccer or football skills. I use this as an example because athletes' skills are specific to their own disciplines. Warriors historically in Japan and elsewhere have required broader skill sets than athletes. They didn't need to be the best at a limited set of skills. They had to be better than most people at many skills. The historical ninja was a figure that had to adapt quickly in order to survive. By focusing more on principles rather than techniques, *Budo Taijutsu* remains a versatile art that encourages one to improvise and think on one's feet.

This book attempts to put in pictures and words something that can only be expressed through motion. Frames were used in this book that visually illustrated principles of movement well in some ways, but yet they give no indication of timing or other dimensions. Books can emphasize or clarify only certain aspects of this art, but the art itself cannot be learned from a book. It cannot be learned from a video, and it cannot actually be learned from watching others in person. It can only be learned from direct contact with students who have actually felt the techniques from *Soke Masaaki Hatsumi* or his direct students. Books, videos and in person observations are helpful, but without a good teacher to transmit the feeling of the *Taijutsu*, a person will only be mimicking what he or she sees and miss much of the nuance that characterizes this art.

Finally, I would like to thank the wonderful teachers I have had that include not only *Soke Hatsumi* and his students Richard Van Donk and Ron Blackwood but also many other instructors and students who have educated me. I would also like to thank all of my students who have helped in the making of this book including John Berry, Tyler Clum, Jared Downing, Anzor Gurashvili, Oscar Ortega, and Jorge Varela.

Introduction

The Origins of Ninjutsu

In one of the oldest scrolls on military strategy written by Fujibayashi Yasutake in 1676, the origins of *Ninjutsu* is explained. This scroll is called the *Bansenshukai* meaning "All Rivers Join the Sea." It explains that in the classical Chinese text *The Art of War* by *Sun Tzu* that information gatherers were used in warfare. It also goes on to explain that *Ninjutsu* started as a military strategy with Emperor Fushigitei. The word *nin* which is also pronounced *shinobi* is written with the Chinese character (忍). This character is made of two parts. The top is a blade (刃) over the word for heart (心). This is pronounced *yaiba kokoro* in Japanese. The words together suggest a warrior's strong spirit. Another way to interpret this word is its meaning "to bear or to endure." This interpretation comes from the idea of one bearing the pain of a knife to the heart. The word has also become synonymous with stealth most likely because of the cunning of historical *ninja*.

Page from the Bansenshukai which is a manual on Ninjutsu written in 1675. This page discusses divination and cosmology.

The Historical Ninja

Credible exploits of *ninja* are limited. After all, *Ninjutsu* was practiced clandestinely. Ninja clans were secretive for their own survival. These clans represented a threat to the powers that be for a variety of reasons. The primary reason perhaps is that *ninjas* were assassins and mercenaries at certain times in history. They were hired in some cases to enact revenge or theft, and were therefore feared and despised. Strangely, although the *ninja* were hated, they served an important function. *Ninja* would be used alone or in small groups to gather information, set fires, and get in behind enemy lines for sabotage. The skills of the *ninja* were needed on certain occasions to supplement what the *samurai* either could not do or would not do. Since the *samurai* were held in high esteem, there were certain jobs that were beneath them. *Ninja* were hired for such jobs and as a result made the difference between success and failure for the objectives of warlords.

Ninja were said to be the descendents of *tengu*. *Tengu* are mythical creatures that were half human and half crow. Originally, the belief came from China from a mythological creature called *tiengou* meaning "heaven dog." In the Shinto religion *tengu* were spirits and homage was paid to them. Buddhism treated these creatures as malicious evil spirits. It was well known that *tengu* possessed special supernatural abilities such as the ability to fly. They were also said to be able to change into other forms, disappear and invade one's dreams. They were also not above playing practical jokes. Their martial arts prowess was also well known well known. Stories of *tengu* teaching martial artists deep in the forest were common place.

The appearance of *tengu* has changed over the centuries. Originally, they appeared to look more like crows and over time they have come to look more like humans with long noses, and wings. *Tengu* are sometimes pictured wearing the garb of Shugendo priests. These priests, which are sometimes called *yamabushi*, practice an esoteric form of Buddhism similar to *Shingon* and *Tendai* sects. These sects are some of the oldest sects in Japan, and *mudra* and *mantra* are commonly used in their religious practices. These monks have a history of going deep into the mountains and undergoing rigorous ascetic training.

It is not improbable that superstitious travelers in the mountains had from time to time come into contact with training *yamabushi*, and because of fear and exaggeration, perpetuated the mystique of both *tengu* and *yamabushi*. Many *ninja* lived in mountainous regions of Japan in clans. Also, many ninja were said to be able to disappear and possess supernatural abilities. It is no wonder that stories of ninja being descendents of tengu arose.

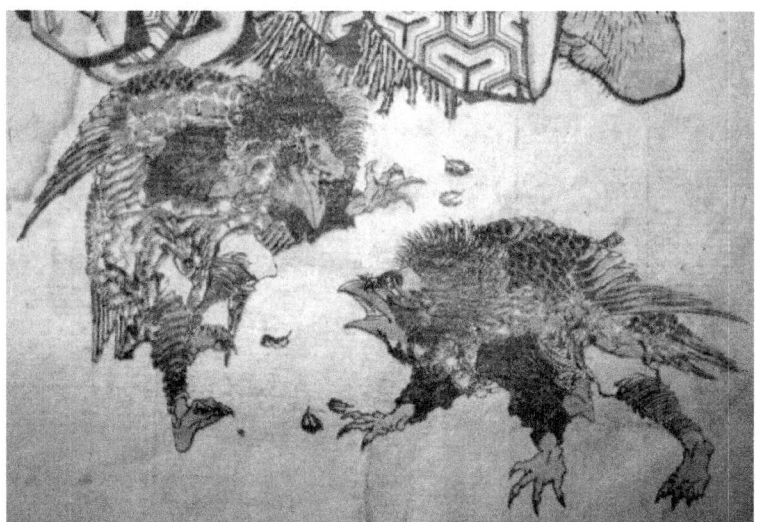
A picture showing two tengu by Hokusai (1760-18490

Ninja families passed on their knowledge of spying, infiltration, and assassination within their own families. There was not really any attempt to take in people seeking to be *ninja* since they were considered as lowly undesirables. Once born into a *ninja* family, one became a ninja and learned the skills of one's ancestors. Training for *ninja* started as a young age as it did for *samurai*. As children they would start learning unarmed combat (*taijutsu*), as well as the use of weapons. Because the skills of the ninja encompassed far more than fighting other skills were learned that were more extensive than what *samurai* learned. Knowledge of how to survive and live off off the land was necessary. *Ninja* had to be resourceful because they often traveled light. The ability to improvise was essential to their survival. Because *ninja* used whatever means necessary to survive and complete their missions, they were considered dishonorable. A *ninja* was supposed to tolerate unbearable humiliation and suffering in the service of others.

Japan has historically been very rural. Although there were different classes, the majority of ninja families were farmers who had to sustain themselves through their own labor. The picture on the next page shows how farmers would have dressed in the 1800's. Their way of life was modest to say the least. This dispels a common misconception regarding how *ninja* dressed. As farmers they would have dressed as any other farmer because to do otherwise would have drawn attention. As farmers, *ninja* clans would have produced strong, able bodied men and women with an intimate knowledge of the land and weather patterns. What they may have lacked in terms of education they made up for in common resourcefulness and common sense.

Japanese peasant farmers in the 1800's

    Although *ninja* were thought of as cold blooded assassins, they were much more adept at espionage. This required a sophisticated understanding of each class of people they would represent. This probably required less worldly knowledge as one might expect and more of an understanding of human nature.

    Because so little was known about *ninja* even in their own time, many myths have grown out of people's fear and superstitions. Notions that *ninja* could fly or disappear were perpetuated as a result of amazing displays of skills and perhaps by exaggerating the abilities of *ninja*.

Ninja by Hokusai 1760-1849

Ninjutsu Today

In modern times the skills of the ninja have all but been lost. Currently, Grandmaster *Masaaki Hatsumi* of Noda City Japan is the inheritor of nine surviving lineages. At one time there were hundreds of lineages of *Ninjutsu*, but most of these lineages have died out. These systems were taught in secrecy or taught under the guise of being something else. With the introduction of *Judo* in Japan, many older systems of Japanese martial arts, particular various styles of *Jujutsu*, faded away from public recognition. With the acceptance of everything new and a decline in interest of the "old ways," traditional Japanese arts shrank in popularity and demand. Another factor was that there was no longer a need for samurai much less *ninja*. It was during these times that Grandmaster *Hatsumi's* teacher *Soke Takamatsu Toshitsugu* was born.

Ninjutsu as it is currently taught by Grandmaster *Masaaki Hatsumi* for the most part does not focus on the skills of the *ninja* outside of hand to hand combat methods and weapons training. The techniques that are taught by Grandmaster *Hatsumi* are however the authentic fighting skills of at least some *ninja* including the famous *ninja Momochi Sandayu*. Two ommon misconceptions come to mind with regard to people's expectations regarding *Ninjutsu* as it is taught by Grandmaster *Hatsumi*. First, some people inquire about training and think that they will learn the skills that they see have seen in a "*ninja* flick." Secondly, some people come with the preconceived idea that *Ninjutsu* is only a martial art and nothing else. Both of these misconceptions contain half truths.

Ninjutsu is a word not commonly heard among people who currently train under Grandmaster *Hatsumi* or his students. Grandmaster *Hatsumi* or *Soke Hatsumi* as he is normally called, has changed the name of what he teaches over time. He originally called what he taught *Togakure Ryu*. This is one of the nine lineages he inherited as a *soke* (inheritor). This *ryuha* (lineage) however did not encompass all of the lineages he taught. He then changed the name to *Ninpo Taijutsu*. This name basically referred to a combat method of the *ninja*. *Soke Hatsumi* has since begun to call the arts he teaches *Budo Taijutsu*. This name is perhaps the most accurate because it refers less to *ninja* skills and more to martial arts in general. *Budo* means "the martial way" and *taijutsu* means "old style hand to hand combat." Although all of the arts *Soke Hatsumi* teaches were practiced by *ninja*, some were practiced more by *ninja* than others and some were not exclusive to *ninja* only. Therefore, the current name is probably the most fitting.

Soke Hatsumi is an iconoclast in many respects. He's the *soke* of nine different lineages extending back over 1100 years and yet he changes the name of what he chooses to teach at a whim. *Soke Hatsumi* adopted the wearing of black uniforms rather than traditional attire typically worn while his teacher was alive. He has taught non-Japanese and has spread what was previously kept secret all over the world. Finally, he has taken the emphasis off of the less sensational aspects of ninja and focused on *Budo Taijutsu* as primarily a martial art and means of self-development. In short, *Soke Hatsumi* has generously shared his art with the world and has made what was secret accessible. Besides being a phenomenal martial artist and teacher, *Soke Hatsumi* is an accomplished writer, artist and musician.

Gyokko Ryu Kosshijutsu

This book will focus on two of the nine lineages which were discussed earlier. They are *Gyokko Ryu Kossijutsu* and *Togakure Ryu Ninpo Taijutsu*. *Soke Hatsumi* has said many times that *Gyokko Ryu Kosshijutsu* forms the "backbone" of the ninja's fighting method. The techniques that form the foundation of this lineage are presented in this book, but it will not cover all of the traditional unarmed techniques. Of the nine lineages, *Gyokko Ryu* is the oldest dating back to around 900 AD. *Gyokko Ryu* is the name of the lineage and *kosshijutsu* describes the method of fighting.

The meaning of *kosshijutsu* is derived from words meaning "the art of bones and fingers." This name most likely comes from the fact that the lineage uses strikes with the thumbs to soft tissue areas that are sensitive on the body. Knowledge of the human body and its meridians presumably led to this method of striking the body. By applying the same amount of power to a much smaller surface area with an attack directed at points on the body, energy could be drained or organs affected. Force would not simply go through the body but resonate as a destructive force internally. These methods were uniquely Chinese but eventually made their way to Japan.

From a historical perspective the existence of *Gyokko Ryu* is extremely unique. No other lineage remains intact to my knowledge in any martial art anywhere in the world. Of course many martial arts trace their roots back to a source, but what is actually practiced has been renamed, reorganized and bears little resemblance to what the original martial art was. *Gyokko Ryu Kosshijutsu* does not fall into this category. The techniques and even their names reflect their origins. It has been passed downed by oral tradition that a person name *Cho Gyokko* or *Yo Gyokko* brought these techniques to Japan. The names are not of Japanese origin. These names are Japanese pronunciations of Chinese words. Another figure, a General *Ibou*, through oral tradition is also credited with bringing this style from China. Little is known about these figures except for the fact that tradition tells us that *Cho* or *Yo Gyokko* may have been a woman who was a member of the royal court. There is no evidence to support this, but this is what has been passed down.

Gyokko Ryu Axiom

"God's Eyes God's Heart"

Gyokko Ryu
Lineage Chart

Ikai (Cho Buren)
Gamon Doshi (Fujiwara Chikadou)
Garyu Doshi
Hachiryu Nyudo
Tozawa Hakuunsai.....*Hogen era 1156-1159*
Tozawa Shosuke.....*Oho era 1161-1162*
Suzuki Saburo Shigeyoshi.....*Joan era 1171-1180*
Suzuki Gobei
Suzuki Kojiro Mitsu
Tozawa Soun.....*Sho o ear 1288*
Tozawa Nyudo Geneai
Yamon Hyoun
Kato Ryu Hakuun.....*Oei era 1394*
Sakagami Goro Katsushige.....*Tembun era 1532*
Sakagami Taro Kunishige.....*Tembun era 1532-1555*
Sakagami Kotaro Masahide.....*Tembun era 1532*
Sogyokkan Ritsushi.....*Tembun era 1532*
Toda Sakyo Ishinsai.....*Tembun era 1532*
Momochi Sandayu.....*Tembun era 1542-1555 (d. 1581)*
Momochi Sandayu II.....*Tensho era 1573-1591*
Momochi Tanba Yasumitsu.....*Bunroku era 1595-1615*
Momochi Taro Saemon.....*Genna era 1615-1624*
Toda Seiryu Nobutsuna.....*Kwanyei era 1624-1644*
Toda Fudo Nobuchika.....*Manji era 1658-1681*
Toda Kangoro Nobuyasu.....*Tenna era 1681-1704*
Toda Eisaburo Nobumasa.....*Hoyei era 1704-1711*
Toda Shinbei Masachika.....*Shotoku era 1711-1736*
Toda Shingoro Masayoshi.....*Gembun era 1736-1764*
Toda Daigoro Chikahide.....*Meiwa era 1764-1804*
Toda Daisaburo Chikashige.....*Bunkwa era 1804*
Toda Shinryuken Masamitsu.....*b. 1824 - d. 1909*
Takamatsu Toshitsugu.....*b. 1887 - d. 1972*
Masaaki Hatsumi.....*b. 1931 – Present*

Calligraphy of Momochi Sandayu
Soke of Gyokko Ryu 1542-1555

"Ninjutsu is not something which should be used for personal desires. It is something which should be used when no other choice is available, for the sake of one's country, for the sake of one's lord, or to escape personal danger. If one deliberately uses it for the sake of personal desires, the techniques will indeed fail totally."

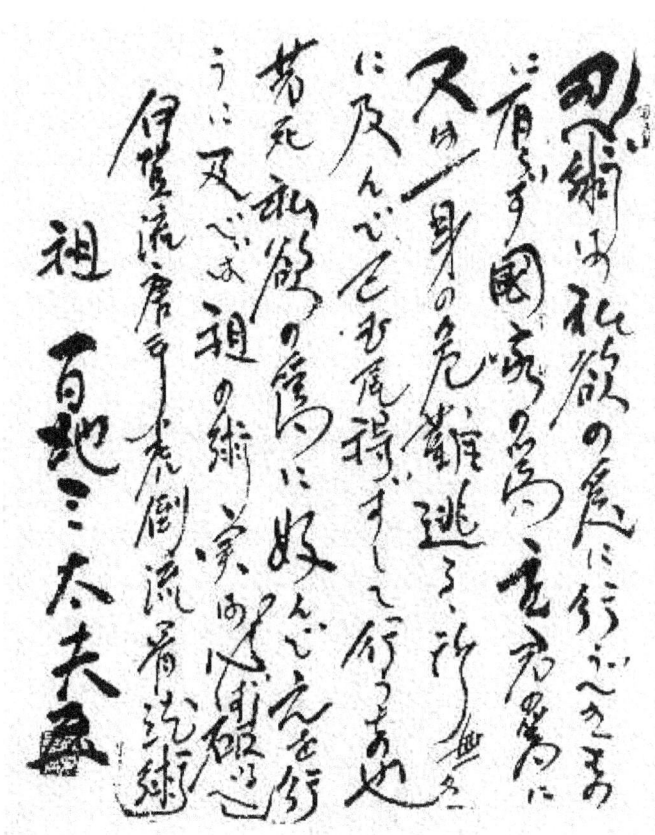

Takamatsu Toshitsugu Soke

Takamatsu Toshitsugu was born on March 10th, 1887 in *Akashi Hyogo* province of Japan. As a boy he was known as *Jitaro*. *Takamatsu Soke* was the grandson of *Toda Shinryuken Masamitsu* who was at the time the head of *Shinden Fudo Ryu*. *Toda* was also a *Soke* of *Koto Ryu*, and *Togakure Ryu*. As a boy *Takamatsu Soke* was frail and weak. He was often teased by classmates. His grandfather made him go to his *dojo* hoping that he would shape up. He was thrown about continuously for a year and was not taught anything. He continued going and finally was stronger and able to learn martial arts. *Takamatsu Soke* had spent time traveling to places like China where he learned various martial arts skills and learned by practical experiences from being challenged in many matches. Takamatsu Soke is a legendary person, but led a very simple life. He had many students as one might imagine, but he chose his students well. He enjoyed walking his dogs daily, painting and of course training. *Takamatsu Soke* passed on the Soke-ship of the nine *ryuha* of the *Bujinkan* to *Masaaki Hatsumi* the current *Soke* of the *Bujinkan* and its *ryuha* (lineages).

Soke Takamatsu Toshitsugu

Masaaki Hatsumi Soke

Masaaki Hatsumi was born in 1931 in Noda City, Japan. In his youth he had an affinity for the martial arts and studied *Judo, Aikido, Karate*, and Western boxing. In the 1950's he met *Takamatsu Toshitsuge*, a master and *soke* of the nine schools of what became the *Bujinkan*. *Soke Hatsumi* had never met anyone like *Takamatsu Soke*, and he believes that by meeting him he began to study true *Budo* for the first time. When *Hatsumi Soke* speaks of *Takamatsu Soke*, he speaks of him with great love and admiration. He was like a father to him.

Many things can be said of *Hatsumi Soke*. Besides being a phenomenal martial artist and teacher, he is also a licensed osteopath, a singer, painter and writer. He has been given many honors and awards throughout his life for his accomplishments not only in Japan but throughout the world. To all members of the *Bujinkan*, *Soke* is our leader and inspiration. To those students who have gone to Japan, he has been very hospitable and has shared his arts generously with the world.

Soke Masaaki Hatsumi and the Author

Gassho no Kamae
Praying Hands Posture

詞語波羅大光明

    Gasshou means "united hands." This is a hand position for reverence, contemplation and respect. One generally sits in *seiza* (sitting on the heels) to do *Gasshou* or sometimes it may be done standing. Training sessions begin with the class lining up in *seiza* (sitting Japanese style) facing the *kamidana* (school shrine). The teacher and students do *Gasshou* and say *Shiken Haramitsu Daikomyo*. This is roughly translated as "Words of Paradise's Brilliant Light." This reminds us that training in for refinement of our body, mind and spirit for a higher good. The Japanese shown above reads *Shiken Haramitsu Daikomyo*.

Hokojutsu
The Art of Stalking

This art is based on distance, angles and timing. All of this naturally arises from movement and not techniques

Perhaps this is the only book on *Ninjutsu* that has ever started with walking. There is a very practical reason for this. *Ninjutsu* is an art based on movement. *Ninjutsu* in the historical sense was not, contrary to popular belief, a martial art. *Ninja* were employed for various purposes including, spying, assassination, and gathering information to name only a few. The very nature of their job dictated that they go unnoticed. If discovered they would need to quickly get away. If caught they would certainly face torture and death. Fighting would have been avoided if possible to avoid detection.

Gyokko Ryu is a lineage that forms the backbone if you will of the ninja fighting method. *Togakure Ryu*, according to *Soke Hatsumi*, arose from *Gyokko Ryu*. *Togakure Ryu* was established approximately 200 years after *Gyokko Ryu* techniques had come to Japan. *Togakure Ryu's* complete name is *Togakure Ryu Ninpo Taijutsu*. These words mean "The Hidden Door Lineage that is the Fighting Art of Stealth Methods." *Togakure Ryu* unlike *Gyokko Ryu* is filled with many methods to avoid detection or get away from attackers who have discovered you. These methods involve various ways to jump, roll, swim and walk.

Students nowadays tend to start learning *Ninjutsu* by learning the *kamae* or postures first. Students are reminded that these are not static positions, but rather snapshots of movements that are constantly changing. As a result, most students practice fighting techniques in which a person stands in *kamae* across from them and attacks. How one moves within distance of such an engagement or how one leaves such an engagement, should be covered early on.

Methods of walking to close the distance or to get away are essential. Students should practice the side-walking method presented here frequently. From these walking methods you will see how the kamae (postures) of this art naturally arise from the *yoko aruki* walking method.

横歩き

Yoko Aruki (Side Walking)

To begin, stand as shown in the first picture so that the body is turned sideways (flat) and the front foot is point straight ahead. Hold the arms out to the sides naturally. Remember tension is unnatural. Step forward with the back leg so that is crosses in front of the front leg. When the legs are crossed, the head and torso are centered over the feet. You may cross your arms in front of you as if doing *Jumonji no Kamae* which will be taught later in this book. As you step forward with the left foot again, you may continue looking forward or you may turn your head to look behind you and bring your arms again to the starting position. Continue repeating this motion of crossing the arms and legs and looking to the front, sides and back as you proceed forward.

This walking method includes some very basic fundamentals of movement. The most obvious is that the upper body (core) remains straight and relaxed while movement is generated by a rolling shift of weight using the legs. This is typical of all movements and posture that will be learned later.

Points to remember:

Keep your back and head straight.
Go slowly at first and shift your weight forward to advance.
Keep your front foot pointed straight ahead.
Keep your other foot pointed to the side.
The head should not rise or fall but stay at the same level.
Done slowly you can learn to walk very quietly.
Done at medium speed you will be able to advance or retreat smoothly while keeping a narrow profile.
Done briskly you will be able to run forward quickly.

A Foundation For Movement

The *kamae* of *Gyokko Ryu* are essential to form a strong foundation. Practice these *kamae* with the knees bent and the hips opened wide. At first these postures will be very uncomfortable and even awkward, but over time they will feel more natural. Discomfort is a sign that one is building muscles that will eventually result in a strong and stable foundation. Change from one posture to another with little or no wasted movement. This takes a lot of practice, but it will pay off later. Knowing the postures is not enough. One must move in them naturally at all times while performing techniques without thinking about them. Without these postures, one will not be in the correct positions for other material that will follow. Make sure that the lead foot always points to the opponent and that the lead hand is directed with intent at the opponent's eyes or heart. Keep the back straight and direct the head forward towards the opponent.

一文字の構え
Ichimonji No Kamae
Straight Posture

From a natural standing position step back with the right foot and raise both arms out in front of you. About 60 percent of your weight should be on the back leg and about 40 percent on the front leg. The rear foot should point to the rear and to the right. The hips are opened widely. Both knees are bent. The front foot should point directly at the opponent. The left hand is extended. The fingers of this hand are closed but not firmly. The left hand points to the opponent's heart, eyes or shoulder. The left elbow is flexed slightly. The right hand forms a *shuto* (knife hand). The outer edge of the right hand rests in the bend of the left elbow with the thumb standing up. Keep the back and head straight. The eyes are focused forward at the enemy's brow. Make sure that the left hand and left foot line up and are directed at the opponent. Practice the same way on both sides. The body is lined up straight making a narrower target for the enemy. Your weight is distributed solidly over your legs and your torso is set back to avoid incoming attacks. Safely distance yourself for a moment.

十文字の構え
Jumonji No Kamae
Cross Posture

From a natural standing position step to either the left or the right side so that the feet are slightly wider apart than shoulder width. Raise both arms in front of the chest so that they are crossed in front of the chest. The hands are held in fists with the thumbs sticking up towards the sky. The back of the fist are exposed to the opponent's view. Another variation is to step back with the right foot with the feet positioned the same way as *Ichimonji no Kamae*. Look straight ahead at the opponent and keep the back straight.

飛鳥の構え
Hicho No Kamae
Flying Bird Posture

From a natural standing position step back slightly with the right foot and raise the left foot so that the arch of the foot rests below the knee on the top of the calf of the right leg. Point the left knee directly at the opponent. The left hand points to the opponent and the right hand rests at the elbow as explained in *Ichimonji no Kamae*. Bend the right supporting leg slightly and keep the back straight. Look directly at the opponent. Practice this on both sides.

Ichimonji no Kamae, *Jumonji no Kamae* and *Hicho No Kamae* are the three basic kamae of *Gyokko Ryu*. However, there are other *kamae* that are also used. Here are some of the others.

自然の構え
Shizen No Kamae
Natural Posture

Stand naturally with the arms to the sides and feet shoulder width apart. Be relaxed and alert with the knees slightly bent. One's center of balance should go directly through the top of the head and down through the center of the pelvis. From this posture one can freely move to any other.

NINJUTSU: ENDURING LEGACY

初心の構え
Shoshin No Kamae
First Intention Posture

This kamae is the same as *Ichimonji* except that the right hand is held at the right hip in a *boshiken* (thumb fist). A *boshiken* is made by forming a fist and allowing the thumb to rest on the folded index finger protruding slightly forward so that one may strike with the tip of the thumb. Practice on both sides.

平の構え
Hira No Kamae
Flat Posture

From a natural standing position, step out to either side. The legs are bent slightly and are about two feet apart. The hips are opened wide and the feet point slightly out to the sides. The spine and head are aligned over the middle of the pelvis and the arms are extended out to the sides. The fingers are closed with the palms facing the opponent. The arms are horizontal at shoulder height. The eyes look forward attentively at the opponent's brow. Practice stepping out to both sides.

Suggestions for Practicing Kamae

Left and Right
Practice the postures on both sides several times.

Eight Directions
From *Shizen no Kamae* practice each posture so that the lead foot points each of the eight directions. For this exercise it might be a good idea to mark a point on the ground that represents a starting position and use tape to mark off the eight directions. Step out to face each direction.

Calling Off the Kamae
Have a person familiar with the postures call them off while the person moves into each posture.

Extra Low Kamae
Practice the postures lower than normal to strengthen the legs.

Moving Forward and Back
Practice the postures moving forward and then moving back.

Flow Drill
Practice moving from one posture to another in a seamless flow.

Once the basic *kamae* are leaned, one must immediately spend a lot of time flowing naturally from one *kamae* to another. The tendency is to learn the *kamae* and then immediately start wanting to learn techniques. Three criteria need to be met while using *kamae* before one can start moving in them properly. The first is breathing. Whether one is static or moving, one must be able to breathe naturally in *kamae*. I recommend doing each *kamae* slowly and using three different breathing methods to do each *kamae*. Breathe naturally, and don't hold your breath.

The second point is relaxation. As one slowly stands in *kamae* all tension must be released from the body. That means the *kamae* cannot be rigid or stiff. This is the second most common mistake I've seen and done when learning *kamae*. Standing in *kamae* for a while will show you where you are holding tension. The third point is that the *kamae* need to be natural. If your leg is shaking from muscular stress as you are doing the *kamae*, it might be a good idea to shorten up the *kamae* a bit. You should not ever have the feeling that *kamae* are hard to move from or into.

Another aspect of being natural is that the *kamae* must become a part of your normal movement. If they are not, how can one expect to ever use them in any realistic way? Once these three criteria have been met, one can start moving freely from one *kamae* to the next. As one practices this, again the focus should be to move naturally without pauses in a string of movements.

It should be noted that each student's *kamae* will vary based on height, weight, in some cases age, physical condition and many other factors. Therefore, the feeling of the *kamae* is more important than the exact form. One student may feel completely natural in a *kamae* while another may feel uncomfortable or awkward. To be natural may require that each student make the *kamae* work for his or her own body. Expecting that a beginning student is going to be able to link all of the *kamae* together freely is a little unrealistic. Therefore, the instructor should model ways of moving and the students can copy them. Learning to move in the *kamae* should follow a progression something like this:

1. Students learn the *kamae*.
2. Students follow the teacher's model of movement with *kamae*.
3. Students practice moving on their own.

It is common that *kamae* are practiced facing one direction. Remember that movement must take place in all directions. Start moving in *kamae* by keeping it simple and slow. Begin with these combinations and be sure to turn the body to eventually face all sides:

Set 1
1. Shizen to Ichimonji no Kamae
2. Shizen to Hira no Kamae
3. Shizen to Jumonji no Kamae
4. Shizen to Hicho no Kamae

This concludes the *Shizen* set. This is the most basic. Students should be taught to step back, forward, left, right and back at a 45 degree angle on both sides. This basic directional pattern applies to all other sets discussed later as well.

Set 2
1. Ichimonji no Kamae to Ichimonji no Kamae
2. Ichimonji no Kamae to Hira no Kamae
3. Ichimonji no Kamae to Jumonji no Kamae
4. Ichimonji no Kamae to Hicho no Kamae

As one learns to move from *Ichimonji no Kamae*, some common mistakes can be noticed. First students tend to have difficulty shifting weight properly. By doing this exercise really slow, they can learn how to shift weight from one leg to another efficiently and effortlessly. Foot placement also becomes important. Secondly, students may tend to move their arms too much as they move from a *kamae* like *Ichimonji to Jumonji*. The smallest amount of movement should be focused on. By the way you may add *Shizen no Kamae* to the end of each set if desired.

Set 3
1. Hira no Kamae to Ichimonji no Kamae
2. Hira no Kamae to Hira no Kamae
3. Hira no Kamae to Jumonji no Kamae
4. Hira no Kamae to Hicho no Kamae

Set 4
1. Jumonji no Kamae to Ichimonji no Kamae
2. Jumonji no Kamae to Hira no Kamae
3. Jumonji no Kamae to Jumonji no Kamae
4. Jumonji no Kamae to Hicho no Kamae

Set 5
1. Hicho no Kamae to Ichimonji no Kamae
2. Hicho no Kamae to Hira no Kamae
3. Hicho no Kamae to Jumonji no Kamae
4. Hicho no Kamae to Hicho no Kamae

If an experienced practitioner went through this string of *kamae* in each set, he or she may notice that the movements seem familiar but the combinations may not. There is a simple reason for this. I have yet to see anyone break down all of the possible combinations into a complete chain. Without practicing all of the combinations, certain combinations become more familiar than others. Because technique is derived from these combinations of movements, the potential to discover techniques is hampered.

If one is learning the *kamae* specific to a particular *ryuha* (lineage), one can also follow the pattern mentioned in the sets.

Next, I'd like to go over some specific exercises that are useful for developing the usefulness of the *kamae* as this level of training.

Drill 1-Walking
Walk a few steps in *Yoko Aruki* and see how each of the *kamae* naturally arise from walking. You may start by walking forward. Then practice walking backwards by reversing the steps of *Yoko Aruki*. To do *kamae* like *Hira* and *Hicho no Kamae* use *Yoko Aruki* to walk to either side.

Drill 2-Avoiding
Two students should work together. Each ties the end of a spare *obi* (belt) to his own belt at the center knot. *Uke* does a *tsuki* to the face very slowly as if in slow motion. Tori moves into each of the *kamae* listed in the sets. Tori simply avoids the punches. The purpose of the belt is as follows. First, the belt helps the students to become aware of the proper distancing (*maai*). Second the belt will allow students to physically experience a "center to center" connection. This is important later when students will learn to take a person's balance.

Drill 3-Sticking

Students add one addition to the previous drill and that is to use their hands when appropriate to stick to the attacking arm of the opponent. This does not mean grabbing. It means to simply make contact with the hand. This will develop sensitivity to the Uke's movements.

Belt Drill 4- Blocking

The drill is the same as the first drill except students begin to use various blocks to strike into the punch. The blocks should not be a force conflicting with force block. Try these variations:

1. Crushing strikes as a means to block
2. Passing the punch by
3. Redirecting the punch

Drill 5- Weapons

The drill is the same as the first drill except students use weapons. Try these variations:

1. Uke has a weapon
2. Tori has a weapon
3. Both Uke and Tori have weapons

Vary the weapons so that short and long weapons are used. The combinations are really endless.

Drill 6-Mirror

This drill can be done with or without a belt. The purpose is for Tori to repeat the mirror image of Uke's *kamae*. No punch is used for this exercise. A belt may be helpful to establish correct distancing.

Drill 7-Striking

The Uke attacks with a punch or kick from *Ichimonji no Kamae* or *Shizen*. Uke responds by moving into the *kamae* established by the practice sets. As Tori moves into *kamae*, he strikes Uke as he moves into the empty space to the sides of the attack. This exercise is best practiced by first using the belt to insure proper distancing.

Seiza Kamae Drill

Seiza is the Japanese seated position with the feet under the buttocks. Although the *kamae* will look slightly different from this seated posture, the upper body may be quite similar. Uke and Tori can face each other in *seiza*. Uke will try to attack Tori with a *tsuki* to the face. Tori will respond by avoiding the attacks using *kamae*, sticking, or using strikes as Uke attacks.

Multiple Attacker Kamae Drill

Two Ukes will attack Tori in slow motion with a *tsuki* (punch) to the face. Tori will use *kamae* to evade the attacks. The following variations should be applied as one gains familiarity with the drill:

1. Add attackers one by one as the skill level progresses.
2. Add weapons as the skill level progresses.

Remember to go slowly. If the Tori is not moving at the same speed as the Uke's, or is not moving in *kamae*, there is no benefit to the exercise.

Confined Space Kamae Drill

Try practicing any of the basic drills in a confined space like in a bathroom, closet or restroom stall. See how little space you can use to move around and evade attacks using only *kamae*. This may cause the *kamae* to shorten up a bit. Don't worry. *kamae* must adapt to the situation.

New Ground Kamae Drill

Practice any of the previously discussed basic drills on an unfamiliar training surface. Here are some suggestions:

1. Grass
2. Gravel
3. Wet surfaces
4. Muddy areas
5. Snow
6. Ice
7. Uneven or hilly ground
8. Stairs
9. Carpet
10. Soft Mats
11. Water

Restricted Movement Kamae Drill

One is not always able to move into *kamae* freely because of limitations caused by one's movements being restricted by clothing. Try some of these variations applied to any of the basic *kamae* drills:

1. Wear formal clothing like a suit
2. Wear sandals, heels, or boots
3. Wear pads of any type
4. Life vests
5. Tight Clothing
6. Armor if you have it
7. Backpacks

To experience *kamae* more fully, one needs to experience the possibilities. By doing so, the *kamae* become natural.

Additional Kamae from Other Lineages

There are a few other common kamae that come from other lineages within the Bujinkan that are not from Gyokko Ryu. There are more than just these three, but these are a few of the most common.

The first picture shows Doko no Kamae. The feet are positioned the same way as Ichimonji no Kamae. This posture is from Koto Ryu.

The second posture is Hoko no Kamae. Invite an attack to the belly and then come down on the opponent once he has committed. This posture is also from Koto Ryu.

The last picture is Fudoza. This means an immoveable seat. This kamae is from Shinden Fudo Ryu. The legs are not simply folded. The subject is sitting on his right heel.

足捌き型
Kihon Sabaki Gata
Basic Forms of Footwork

Starting position

Step back and to the right.

Step back and to the left from the starting position.

The *kamae* are not static poses. In order to make them come alive, one must move from *kamae* to *kamae* using the eight directions as is shown in these pictures. Practice moving in the different *kamae* as shown. *Taijutsu* starts first with the *kamae* and how to move in them. What one does with the hands comes later.

Starting position

Step to the left.

Step to the right.

Starting position

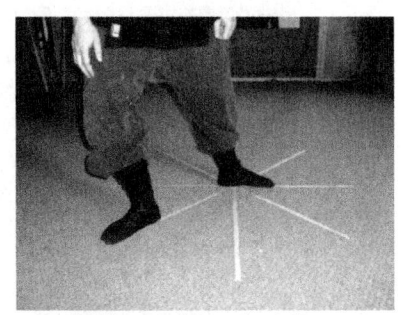

Right step forward as shown.

Left step forward as shown.

Starting position

Step forward and turn to the left.

From the starting position step forward and turn to the right.

Yoko Aruki
Side Step

*From Shizen no Kamae, cross step forward to the left and to the right.
Keep your toes on the front foot pointing forward.*

受身型体変術
Ukemi Gata Taihenjutsu
Forms of Receiving and the Art of Changing the Body

Ukemi refers to ways in which one falls to avoid getting injured. This may include what is typically referred to as breakfalls and rolls. These skills are similar in some ways to gymnastic tumbling exercises. By learning these skills one protects oneself from throws that would ordinarily injure those without training. It is best to think of these forms as ways of receiving an attack by using the body. The ground is used as an ally to set oneself up for a possible counter attack or a means to safely free oneself by rolling away. Try to do these exercises in a quiet manner making as little noise as possible and applying as little force to the ground as possible. When being thrown by an opponent learn to be in control of your own fall and see the openings in the opponent's defenses.

体変受身型
Taihen Ukemi Gata
(Changing the Body to Receive Forms)

前返り (前方回転)
Mae Gaeri (Zenpo Kaiten)
Forward Roll

両手をついて 前方 廻転, 片手を いて前方 廻転, 左右, 手を使わず前方 廻転, 飛鳥 廻転両手づき(空転両手づき前方,片手をづき前方,横転両手をづき横転,片手をづき横転, 廻転--飛び廻転),自然。
Two hand front rolls, one hand front rolls, left and right, rolls in which the hand is not used, flying rolls with both hands (flips in the air--both hands to the front, one hand to the front, side rolls--both hands side roll, one hand side roll, and flying rolls), and natural uses.

Zenpo Kaiten
Forward Roll

Clear away an area of grass so that you can roll in a soft place free of debris. Bend your knees and place your hands down on the ground palms first. The student here is doing a slightly more advanced form in which he places the back of the hands momentarily on the ground before tucking the head and rolling forward. Do not allow your head to touch the ground. When you tuck and roll, only your back will be touching. Do not flop over flat. Keep your back arched throughout the roll.

Zenpo Kaiten
Forward Roll

Naname Zenpo Kaiten
Diagonal Forward Roll

Now try rolling forward diagonally. First find a clear area and stand normally in *Shizen no Kamae*. Step forward and to the right with the right foot. Place the side of your right hand down on the ground so the fingers point between your legs. Bend your front knee and extend your body forward to roll from your right shoulder, across your back and over your left hip. Come up into *Hoko no Kamae* or *Ichimonji no Kamae* as shown in the pictures. Practice rolling forward diagonally on the left and right sides.

Naname Zenpo Kaiten
Diagonal Forward Roll

NINJUTSU: ENDURING LEGACY

NINJUTSU: ENDURING LEGACY

Another View

横返り（左右回転）
Yoko Gaeri
(Sayu Kaiten)
Side Roll

両手をついて側方廻転,片手をついて側方廻転,手を使わず側方廻転,飛鳥廻転(空転,横転,廻転),自然。
Side roll using both hands, side rolling using one hand, side roll without hands, flying rolls (flips, cartwheels, rolling), and natural uses.

Sayu Kaiten
Side Roll

NINJUTSU: ENDURING LEGACY

48

NINJUTSU: ENDURING LEGACY

Oten -Cartwheels

後ろ返し(後方回転)
Ushiro Gaeshi (Koho Kaiten)
Backwards Roll

両手をついて廻転,片手をついて廻転,手を使わず廻転,飛鳥廻転(空転,横転,廻転),自然。
Roll using both hands, roll using one hand, roll without hands, flying rolls (flips, cartwheels, rolling), and natural uses.

  Begin the Backwards Roll by dropping to one's bottom with the right leg extended out in front of you. Roll backwards. Tuck the legs in as you go over your shoulder and come up in kamae. Your head should not touch the ground. As you become more proficient, use only one hand and finally no hands. Later try holding a weapon in the hands.

Koho Kaiten
Backwards Roll

Variation from a Squatting Position

From Shizen no Kamae take a short step back and crouch down.
Roll onto your back and use the momentum to bring your legs over one shoulder.

Bring the left leg forward when coming up and stand up in Ichimonji no Kamae.

Variation

前方受身
Zenpo Ukemi
Forward Breakfall

膝立位にて両手は前方受身,片手前方 受身, 立位前方受身(両手),
受身より突き蹴り,自然。
Front breakfall standing erect on the knees, one hand front breakfall, standing erect front breakfall (both hands), breakfall from a kick or punch, and natural uses.

Students sometimes have a fear of falling and so beginners should stand on their knees and drop forward. This seems less scary and is a way to gradually work students into a standing version. The hands and forearms contact the ground first in a triangular shape to absorb impact over a larger surface area. Also, one's head turns to the side to avoid hurting the face. Later students do this standing by bending the knees to lower the body and then dropping forward to the ground in the same way. One leg is extended up and out from the rear partly for balance and protection. This may be used against a push from behind however rolling may be preferred.

NINJUTSU: ENDURING LEGACY

Zenpo Ukemi
Forward Breakfall

54

Yoko Nagare Ukemi
Side Flowing Breakfall

This picture shows the basic position for falling with *Yoko Ukemi*. This is the safe way to fall on one's side from a joint lock or throw. Notice the correct positioning of the body. The head is up and the chin is tucked to the chest to prevent the head from accidentally hitting the ground. The left hand covers the ribs and vital organs and the body is turned so that one is partially on the side and partially on the back. The legs are positioned in such a way that one's body can absorb the shock of hitting the ground and get up quickly. Having the right hand stretched out can also help to absorb shock and be used to rise. Falling this way is appropriate for beginners. Once a student overcomes any fear of falling, he can learn to fall covering the head or holding weapons.

Koho Ukemi
Rear Breakfall

Stand in *Shizen no Kamae*. Take a small step back with the right leg and lower your body by bending your knees. Don't bend forward at the waist. Sink down and roll back onto your back in a smooth rocking motion.

Shown here is the advanced version. Notice that the hands are not used. The hands are held up to protect the head from a further attack. Also, notice the position of the legs. This is to protect the groin. Beginners may use two hands as they go down. If two hands are used, one should make sure not to fall on the hands and then rock back. This could cause injury. Beginners may also find it easier to just rock back and keep the legs out and not protect the groin as shown. In the beginning the main concern is to fall back smoothly and safely onto the back. Lastly, make sure the head is up off the ground so a head injury is prevented, and don't slap your hands.

四方 天地 飛び
Shihou Tenchi Tobi
(Four Directions, Heaven and Earth Leaping)

高く飛ばず 低く幅を行くこと四方 にあり。
Jump lower at a greater span than high and in all four directions.

天地の天は雲 にあり地 は流れにあり。
The heaven of heaven and earth is in the clouds and the earth is in the flowing.

When jumping up to avoid an attack to both legs keeps your feet tucked under your bottom to get maximum height.

Tenchi Tobi
Heaven and Earth Jump

Bend the knees, jump up and fold the feet under you.

Jump straight up crossing the feet under the buttocks. This is used to avoid something swung at the legs.

Zenpo Tobi
Leaping Forward

Koho Tobi
Leaping Back

Yoko Tobi
Leaping to the Side

Dakentaijutsu
The Art of Striking

Tsuki
Thrust Punch

Variation 1

Stand in *Shizen no Kamae*. Be completely relaxed and then step forward and strike. Do not chamber the punch. Simply make a straight path from wherever your hand is to whatever you are trying to hit. Hold your other hand up for protection. Remember that the shortest distance between two points is a straight line. Don't make sudden jerking movements as this will be telegraphed to the opponent. Move naturally, quietly and smoothly. Thrust with your whole body through the target. This punch should be like a battering ram. Don't straighten your arm completely. Keep the bones of the forearm aligned with the bones of the fist. Punch with the intention to topple what you are hitting. Release energy and don't tighten your muscles to gain strength. By turning your chest to the side you can increase the distance.

Variation 2

Stand in *Ichimonji no Kamae*. Shift your weight to your front leg. Step forward with your right leg and punch as described above. Do this in a rolling motion forward. Practice both sides for every technique shown in this book. Again, always remember to punch with your whole body and not just your arms or shoulders. This is a powerful punch, especially from *Ichimonji no Kamae*. Variation 1 and 2 are beginning punches that encompass the fundamentals of our movements. They represent only a small representation of the possible ways to strike an opponent.

Points to Remember

Don't lean to far forward on the front leg.
Don't drop your hands. Keep them up.
Don't scrunch up your shoulders

Keep your back relatively straight.
Keep your fist, shoulder, knee and foot in alignment.
Keep your left shoulder back.

Tsuki
Thrurst Punch

Jodan Uke
Upper Block

Jodan Uke mean an upper position block. The word *Uke* here means to receive an attack. To begin start from *Ichimonji no Kamae* as shown on the next page squared off with your training partner. As the *Uke* steps forward and commits to his attack, step back and to the right using the right foot to get the body off of the line of attack. More than anything else, this is the most important point. At the same time keep make a fist with the left hand and raise the left forearm up under the incoming punch's arm. The left forearm should be at a 45 degree held up like a Roman shield. The *Uke's* punch will continue forward but will be too high to make contact. The right hand can stay in place or move up to guard the right side of the head. This is the most simple form of *Jodan Uke* and should be learned first by beginners because it takes the least amount of precision and coordination.

Variations

1. The Circular Block
As you step back and to the right to block, allow the left elbow to freely move the hand in a counterclockwise circle as you strike the *Uke's* right inner forearm with the back of your left knuckles. This should be practiced next as it takes more precision to strike the forearm than it does to just avoid the attack.

2. The Striking Block
As you step back and to the right to block, keep the left hand in front of you but turn the hips and shoulders away from the attack. With a snap of the hips using coiled energy from the spine and legs, strike swiftly with the left fist into the *Uke's* punching arm knocking it away to the side. Don't let your own fist go out to the side. Keep your fist pointed at the training partner after striking away his punch and be ready to counter-attack. This type of block is referred to a *Jodan Nagashi* or *Uke Nagashi*. Nagashi refers to a flowing motion. Certainly this block is harder because it takes precision to strike the forearm very exactly, but also requires more coordination to correctly move the entire body to strike effectively as an entire unit.

3. The Rising Block
As you step back and to the right to block, use the left fist to strike upwards under the bones of the attacker's right elbow joint. This is sometimes delivered with a sudden bump forward to imbalance the adversary. This takes considerable skill and precision; however, it is devastating and can render the attacker's arm useless.

(*The picture shown on the following page shows a basic Jodan Uke from Shizen no Kamae shot in real time. Notice that the student is stepping back and is keeping his right hand up to guard against a possible second punch.*)

Jodan Uke
Upper Block

Gedan Nagashi
Lower Flowing Block

When an attacker attempts to kick you with a right front kick, immediately step off line forward and to the right with the right foot to avoid getting hit. Sweep the left hand in a fist back and to the side hitting the kick or brushing it by you. Avoid striking the attacker's leg directly at a 90 degree angle with the wrist or forearm. It could easily result in injury. Notice that if you allow the kick to sail past you, the *Uke* will keep coming forward and his head will be dangerously exposed to a counter-attack. Timing is everything so one should not move until the kick is launched otherwise you will be tracked and then struck. The same holds true for avoiding any type of attack. Notice how the pinky side of the left fist is turned up when striking the kicking leg. Pay attention to this and all of the other details of the picture.

Gedan Nagashi
Lower Flowing Block

NINJUTSU: ENDURING LEGACY

三心の型
Sanshin no Kata
The Three Hearts Forms

The *Sanshin no Kata* can be roughly translated as Three Hearts Form. However, the word *shin* (心) could also be translated as mind or spirit. So, one could say that these forms require all of one's heart, mind and spirit. Another interpretation is that these forms represent the heart, mind and spirit of *Gyokko Ryu* and *Budo* (Martial Arts) in general.

The *Sanshin* forms are generally practiced alone and not with a partner. They contain the basic postures, blocks, strikes and kicks. More importantly they contain the basic movements of *Gyokko Ryu* and for that matter *Ninjutsu*, in general. Practice these forms over and over and learn to eliminate any wasted movement. Practice each form with an economy of motion and notice how the hand and foot always move together as one shifts one's body forward or back. They function as a means to study the biomechanical movements of our *Taijutsu*.

地の型
Chi No Kata
The Earth Form

始め自然体。右向けの体勢よ,右手三指を突き出すのと右足を出すのと同時に。次に,左手の三指を出すのと左足を出すのと同時に。三指の根の根本に親指が横にいっぱいの型。引いた左手は拳,親指を立てた拳。引いた左手は拳,親指を立てた拳。

Begin in a relaxed and natural posture. From a posture facing the right, three fingers are projected out at about the same time the right leg is put out. Next, the left three fingers go out about the same time as the left leg goes out. The thumb is on the side of the base of the three fingers. The thumb is erected on the left hand that drew back.

The way that this form is typically practiced is as follows. From a natural standing position, step back with the right foot and extend the left hand out in *Shoshin no Kamae*. Begin moving the closed right fist at your right hip back behind you forming a *Sanshiten Ken*. See the section of this book called the Hiken Juruppo for a close up if necessary. Shift your weight forward over your left foot and then step forward with your right foot striking upwards at the same time in a rolling motion.

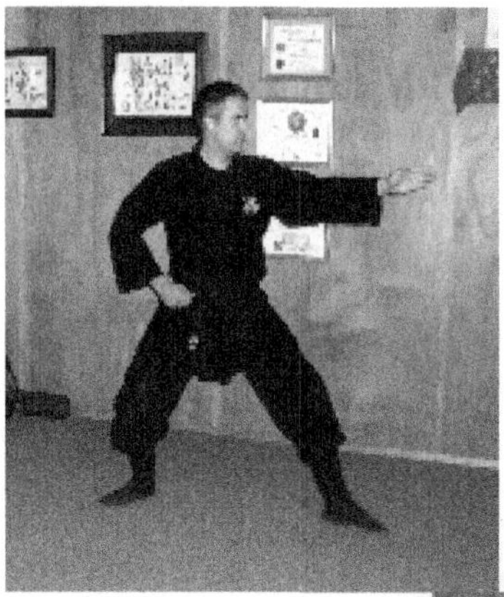

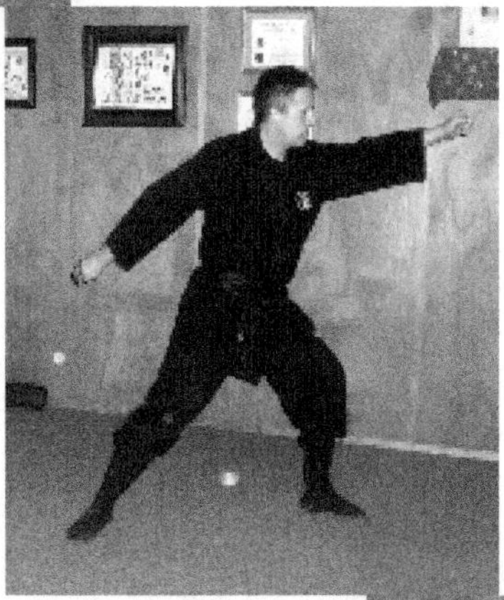

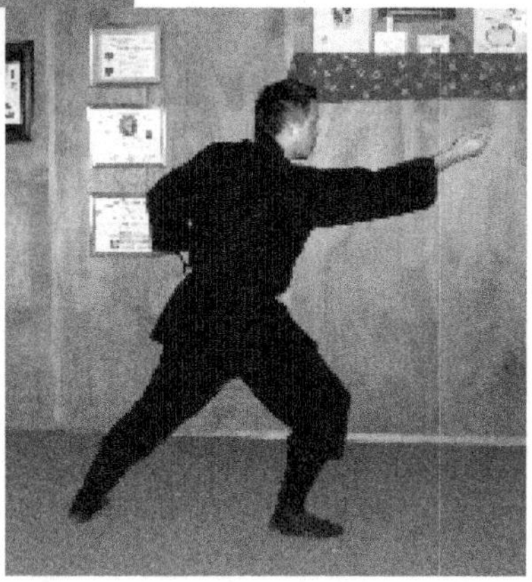

NINJUTSU: ENDURING LEGACY

水の型
Sui No Kata
The Earth Form

自然体。右足を引いて左手は左足前方に。左手は真っ直ぐに手刀を出し、右手は自分の右側帯の辺に親指を立て右拳の型。受身。手刀打ち（拳を上に向ける）。左技のこと。これを三回 繰り返す。

Natural Posture. The right leg draws back and the left hand is in front of the left leg. The left hand is straight out in a shutou, my right hand is at my own belt area with the thumb standing up. Block. Knife hand strike (the fist is facing up). The technique is the same on the left. Repeat this three times.

Start in *Shoshin no Kamae* with the left hand and left foot forward. Begin stepping back and to the right slightly as if getting off line of an attack. Make a *Jodan Uke* with the left arm and raise the right hand in a fist at the right side of the head. Shift your weight forward to the front left leg and then step forward with the right foot. At the same time suddenly turn the right fist and open it in a strike with the palm up. This strike is *Omote Shuto* (Outer Knife) and the name of the fist is *Kiten Ken* (Turning Fist). See the *Hiken Juruppo* section of this book for details on this fist and any others. Do this the same way on both sides and repeat each set three times.

NINJUTSU: ENDURING LEGACY

NINJUTSU: ENDURING LEGACY

火の型
Ka No Kata
The Fire Form

自然体°　右足を引いて左手は左足前方に°　左手は真っ直ぐに手刀を出し，右手は自分の右側帯の辺に親指を立て右拳の型°　受身°　手刀打ち（拳を下に向ける）°　左技のこと°　これを三回　繰り返す°

Natural Posture. The right leg draws back and the left hand is in front of the left leg. The left hand is straight out in a shutou, my right hand is at my own belt area with the thumb standing up. Block. Knife hand strike (the fist is facing down). (Means the technique on the left is same). Repeat this three times.

From *Shizen no Kamae* step back and to the right into *Shoshin no Kamae*. Make a *Jodan Uke* block with the left arm and raise the right fist to the right side of the head. Shift your weight forward to the front leg and then step forward with the right foot. As you step strike down opening the right fist with the palm down. This strike is *Ura Shuto* (Inner Knife) and the name of the fist is *Kiten Ken* (Turning Fist). Do this the same way on both sides and repeat each set three times.

NINJUTSU: ENDURING LEGACY

NINJUTSU: ENDURING LEGACY

風の型
Fu No Kata
The Wind Form

自然体｡ 構え｡ 下段受け｡ 親指を立てた拳にて右突き型｡ 左技のこと｡ これを三回繰り返す｡

Stand naturally. Assume a kamae. A low block. A right thrust with thumb extended on the fist. The technique is the same on the left. Repeat this three times.

From *Shizen no Kamae* step back into *Shoshin no Kamae* with the left hand forward and the right hand in a fist at the right hip. Step slightly back and to the right with the right foot and then make a left *Gedan Uke* (lower block) with the left fist. Shift your weight to the front leg and then step forward delivering a waist-level strike with the thumb. This is called a *Boshiken* (thumb fist) or *Shitoken* (finger sword fist). Do this the same way on both sides and repeat each set three times.

NINJUTSU: ENDURING LEGACY

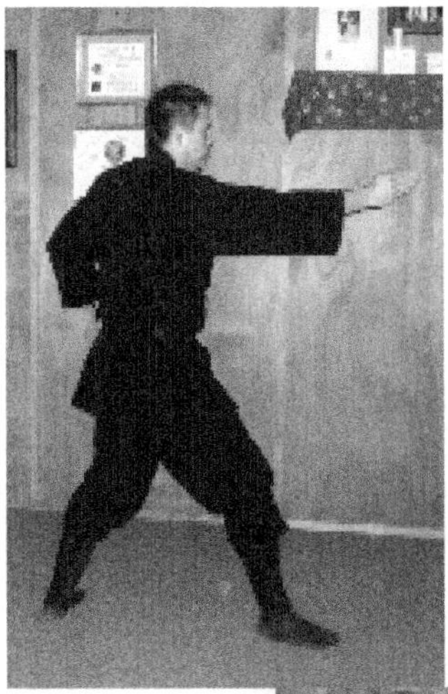

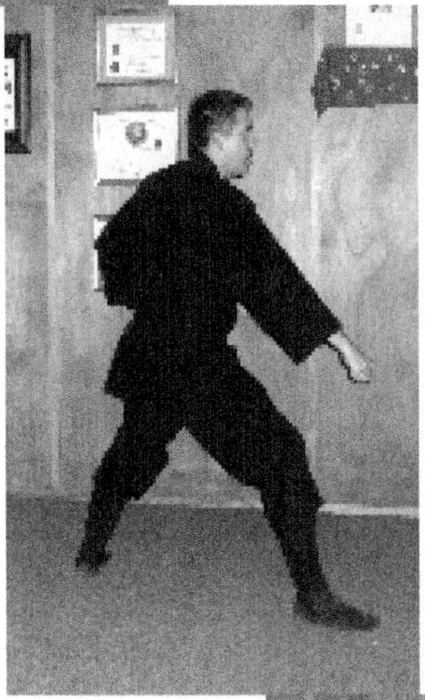

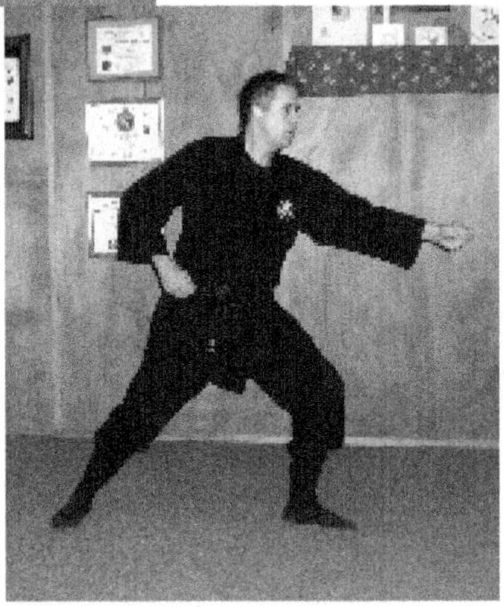

空の型
Ku No Kata
The Emptiness Form

自然体゜構え゜下段受け゜右手を上に揚げると右足を腰を落とし高く蹴る゜左技のこと゜これを三回 繰り返す゜口伝゜窪地 へ 落ちる習いの水なれど，やがては登る初めなりけり゜口伝

Stand naturally. Assume a kamae. A low block. Raise up the right hand, drop the hips, and kick high. The technique is the same on the left side. Repeat this three times. Oral Transmission. (This suggests that essential details can only be passed on by word of mouth from teacher to student.) In life water normally makes its way down to depressions in the ground, but before long it begins to rise. Kuden. Orally transmitted.

From *Shizen no Kamae* step back and to the right with right foot into *Shoshin no Kamae*. Make a *Gedan Uke* (low block) with the left fist. Raise the right hand up with the palm facing forward. Lower the hips and kick high with the right foot using the entire sole.

NINJUTSU: ENDURING LEGACY

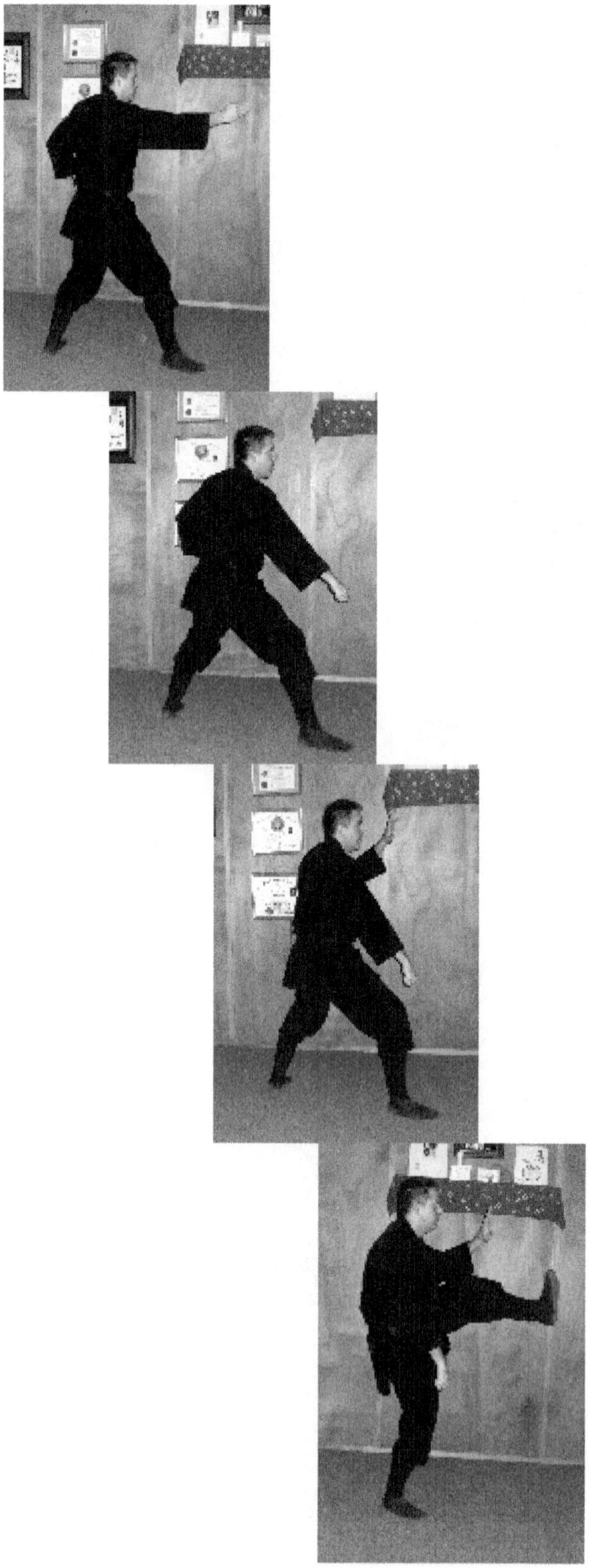

Another View of Chi No Kata

Another View of Sui No Kata

NINJUTSU: ENDURING LEGACY

Another View of Ka No Kata

NINJUTSU: ENDURING LEGACY

Another View of Fu No Kata

Another View of Ku No Kata

After raising up your right hand as a distraction, do a stomp kick with the right foot.

基本八法型
Kihon Happo Gata
The Eight Foundation Forms

骨子三法, 捕手五法, 合わせて 基本八法 と言う。
The Kosshi Sanpo and Torite Goho can be combined together to be called the Kihon Happo.

骨子三法
Kosshi Sanpo
The Essential Three Methods

The *Kosshi Sanpo* put the three basic postures into action against an opponent's punch. These techniques teach how these basic postures are used. Of course there are many variations that can be discovered through their practice. Once these basic forms are learned well, they can be combined with the *Torite Kihon Goho* forms to take down the opponent. Notice the way in which the hands are used to strike the opponent. Two of the techniques use variations of the *Kiten Ken* or "turning fist." In these strikes the outer edge of the hand strikes the neck. In the *Jumonji* form the *Boshi Ken* or "thumb strike" is used against a soft tissue target of the underarm called *butsumetsu*. These kinds of targeted strikes typify *Kosshijutsu*.

右一文字 の 構え
Migi Ichimonji no Kamae
Right One Line Posture

右一文字に構える,右一文字と言うは,右手を前方に出て, 左手は拳と親指を立て,右手の肘関節の上に置くかのごとき構えなり。右手を右に廻し, 腰の方向より左肩に廻す。これを廻すときは必ず拳を変化していること。これは敵の攻撃を砕く意なり。左手を左へ廻し, 拳が半開きとなって, 相手方の右横首筋に打ち込む。左足一歩前進と同時なり。左技のこと。これを八回繰り返す。

Migi ichimonji is called this because the position is a straight line on the right. The right hand is put out to the front, the thumb on the left hand stands up and is put on top of the right hand's elbow joint when one stays in this posture. The right hand rotates to the right and left shoulder rotates from the direction of the hips. When you do that rotation be sure that you have changed the fist. This becomes the feeling that crushes the enemy's attack. The left hand is rotated towards the left, the fist becomes half opened, and hit into the right side of the adversary's neck muscles. The left foot advances a step at the same time while doing this. With regards to the technique on the left side, it is the same and is repeated eight times.

Step back and to the right from *Ichimonji no Kamae* as the *Uke* punches at your face with a right fist. Block with a left *Jodan Uke* and raise your right fist up to your head as you step in and strike his neck knocking the assailant backwards.

(The pictures shown here are the side opposite of what is described here.)

Ichimonji no Kamae

Another View

右飛鳥の 構え
Migi Hicho no Kamae
Right Flying Bird Posture

左足は右足中関節のところに上げ,左手を半開き 前方に右手拳と親指を立てて,左手 の 肘関節の辺 に位取りのこと。左手を左下より右廻し。左腰辺 より 右手 肩 辺 に 位取り 変ず 前 の 通り,拳 に 変わっていること。

The left foot is raised to the right knee joint, the left hand is half opened in front, and the right hand fist's thumb is standing up and is positioned on the elbow joint. From the lower left, the left hand is turned to the right. As before the right hand position transforms from the left hip area to the shoulder and the fist is changed.

From *Hicho no Kamae* block the *Uke*'s right mid-level punch with a left *Gedan Nagashi*. Sequentially, kick up into the *Uke*'s ribs or armpit with a lift kick followed by a right Shuto (knife hand strike) as you step forward knocking him down.

NINJUTSU: ENDURING LEGACY

Another View

右十文字の構え
Migi Jumonji no Kamae
Right Cross Posture

左手を内側にして右十文字位取りのこと)。右手拳をそのまま右上に右廻し,右手親指で敵の胸部を突く。右上に手を半開きで右側に上げる。左手拳をそのまま左上に右廻し,左手親指で敵の胸部を突く。左上に手を半開きで左側に上げる。この時, 右手は拳に変わり, 胸部は十文字位取りのこと。左技のこと。

The left hand is positioned on the inside in this case. With the right hand as it is turn the right hand up to the right and thrust into the enemy's chest area with the thumb of the right hand. Raise the half-opened right hand up to the right side. With the left hand as it is turn the left hand up to the left and thrust into the enemy's chest area with the thumb of the left hand. Raise the half-opened left hand up to the left side. Now the right hand alternates and the fists and are at the chest area in a crossed (*jumonji*) position. The technique is the same on the left.

Stand facing the *Uke* in *Jumonji no Kamae* with the left foot forward. The *Uke* will attack by stepping forward with a right punch to the face. Step back and to the right to get off line of the attack and block the attacker's right forearm from the inside with the knuckles of your left fist. Then track up the right arm into the armpit (*butsumetsu*) with a left thumb fist strike by shifting your weight forward over the front leg in a rocking motion. After striking quickly shift back to the starting position.

Jumonji no Kamae

Another View

捕手基本五法
Torite Kihon Goho
The Five Foundational Methods of Capturing

These techniques form the foundation of dealing with an opponent seizing the clothing or grabbing and trying to punch. The opponent will either seize the lapel at the chest or will try and grab the sleeve at the elbow. When an attacker seizes the chest, it likely that he may try to pull or push to set up the distance to punch the face. Seizing the elbow to control an individual by today's standards may seem unusual, but when we consider that in the past many people in Japan were armed with swords we can understand why someone would try to control a person's arm. Imagine if most men today carried a hunting knife or gun.

Omote Gyaku

Outer Reversal

1.

相手方は左手にて片胸を捕る。 我は右手 表を小手逆 捕りに高く上げ, 右足を引く。小手に廻し,下ろす。この際,胸取りの理を口伝す。受けは敵の右手に対て左手を添えること。受けは 敵の右手に対て左手を添えること。左技 のこと。

The adversary seizes the chest with his left hand. I raise my right hand up applying an outer reversal to the wrist and draw the right leg back. Rotate the wrist and take down. In this case, the principles regarding taking the chest are orally transmitted. The left hand block is attached to the enemy's right hand being countered. The technique on the left is same.

Tori and *Uke* face each other in *Shizen no Kamae*. *Uke* steps forward with his left foot and grabs a hold of *Tori's* right lapel. *Tori* immediately steps back and to the left with his left foot and uses his right hand to push away *Uke's* hand to avoid the grab. If grabbed Tori will place his right thumb on the back of *Uke's* grabbing hand and seize his own lapel just below where *Uke* has grabbed him. If grabbed *Tori* will twist the *Uke's* wrist outward and pull the lapel away from his grip. If necessary use the forearm and the strength of the legs to leverage *Uke's* elbow up painfully to weaken his grip. Suddenly *Tori* will step back with the right foot and turn his hips as this helps to turn *Uke's* hand over throwing him on his back.

NINJUTSU: ENDURING LEGACY

104

Another View

Omote Gyaku Men Tsuki
Outer Reversal and Face Punch

2.

相手方は左手にて片胸を捕る。右手で打ち来る。我は左手拳にて受ける。同時に右手にて敵の左手小手を表逆捕り。1のごとく投げる。ここで大事なことは,我は左手で胸捕りし,手を我が右手に添えたものを,敵が左拳に打ち来るを, 右手を中心 に体変す。この 練習第一なり。この 練習第一 なり。左技のこと。

The adversary seizes the chest with his left hand. A right hand is used to come in with a punch. I block with a left-handed fist. At the same time capture the enemy's left wrist in an outer reversal (*omote gyaku*) with the right hand. Throw like number one. The most important thing here is to move the body with the right hand at one's core and attached to the hand that has grabbed the chest as the enemy's left fist comes to hit. This becomes the first practice. The technique is the same on the left side.

Tori and *Uke* face each other in *Shizen no Kamae*. *Uke* steps forward and seizes *Tori's* right lapel with his left hand and attempts to punch him in the face without stepping with his right fist. Once grabbed *Tori* lightly covers *Uke's* left hand with his right hand and places his right thumb on the back of his hand. *Tori* will immediately step back and to the right after *Uke* has begun to punch blocking the right *Tsuki* with a left *Jodan Uke*. *Tori* then turns his hips to the right in a spiraling motion and uses his contact with the left hand and right forearm of *Uke* like a large wheel turning *Uke* over on his back with a throw.

NINJUTSU: ENDURING LEGACY

Ura Gyaku

Inner Reversal

3.

相手方 は左手 にて片胸を捕る。我 は敵の左手の表小手を逆に左手にて捕り、左足を引き、小手逆の手下に一度引き、たちまち変化。小手上より廻し、右足を引き,右手にそつて 投げ。左技のこと。

The adversary seizes the chest with his left hand. I suddenly change taking the enemy's left hand with the left hand, drawing back the left leg as a reversal is applied to the wrist. Hold the wrist up as you rotate it, draw the right leg back, and throw with the connection to the right hand. The technique is the same on the left.

(What is described below is the same but on the opposite side)
    Tori and *Uke* face each other in *Shizen no Kamae*. *Uke* steps forward with his right foot and seizes *Tori's* lapel with his right hand. *Tori* steps back and to the left with his left foot to avoid being grabbed. At the moment *Uke* is about to seize the lapel, *Tori* will also intercept *Uke's* right hand lightly placing his right thumb on the back of his hand. If *Tori* is grabbed he will place his left palm over the knuckles of *Uke's* closed fist. As *Uke* hold *Uke's* hand and wrist he will point his right elbow directly at *Uke's* face. *Tori's* feet will be similar to a right foot forward *Ichimonji no Kamae*. If *Uke* tries to punch, *Tori* will have the option of counter-attacking with a *Shuto* to the neck. *Tori* will not attempt to use the strength of the arms of shoulders to twist *Uke's* hand off. *Tori* will simply compress *Uke's* hand close to his body and turn his hips to the right. This hip movement alone will turn over *Uke's* hand so that the pinky side of his fist is facing up. *Uke* loses his form and bends at the waist. As he tries to regain his posture or attempt to strike with the left hand. *Tori* will bring his hips back to the center line and press down on *Uke's* elbow. Make sure the *Uke's* elbow has a slight bend in it. This painfully compresses the radius, ulna and nerve of the forearm in a painful lock. *Tori's* left hand is ready to strike into *Uke's* face at any moment. Pictures here show the other side.

Press down on the elbow to cause severe pain.

Another View

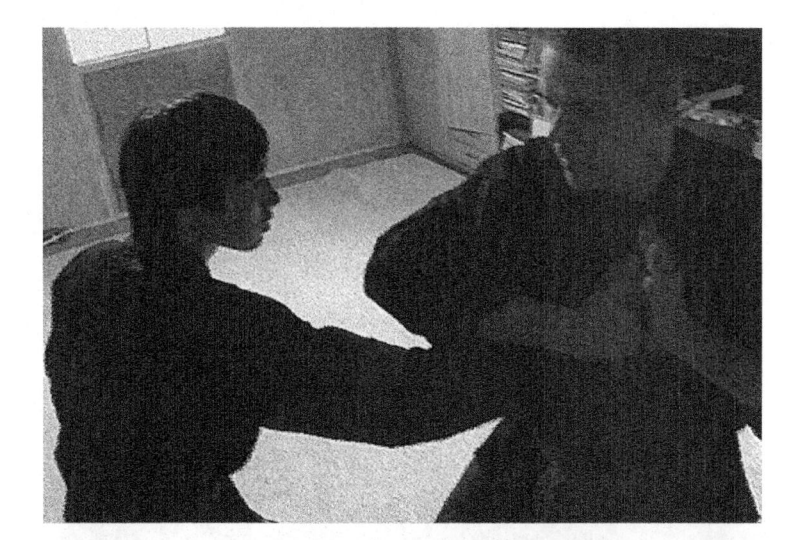

Ura Gyaku Dori as a Throw

Sometimes when the hand is turned over as shown in the previous pictures, Tori will raise Uke's hand up, take it with both hands and then step back to the right to throw Uke forward at a point a few feet out centered between his legs. Uke will go into a roll to avoid injury.

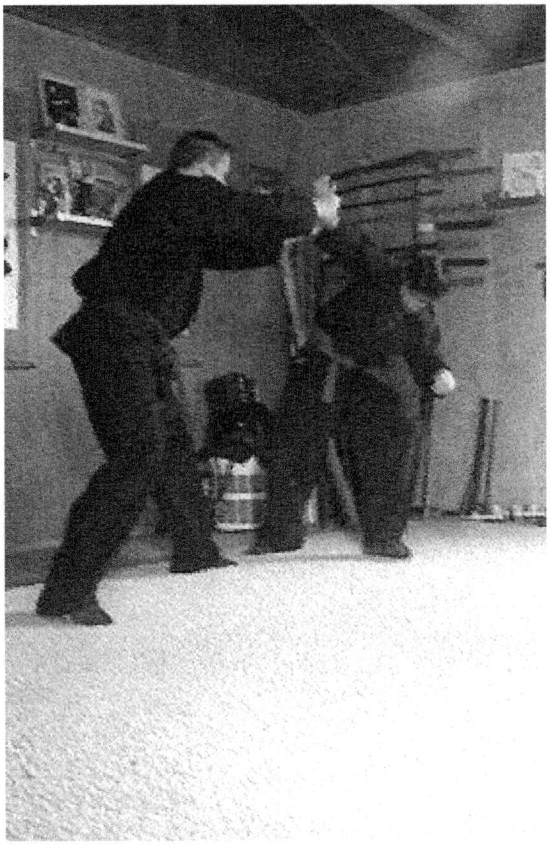

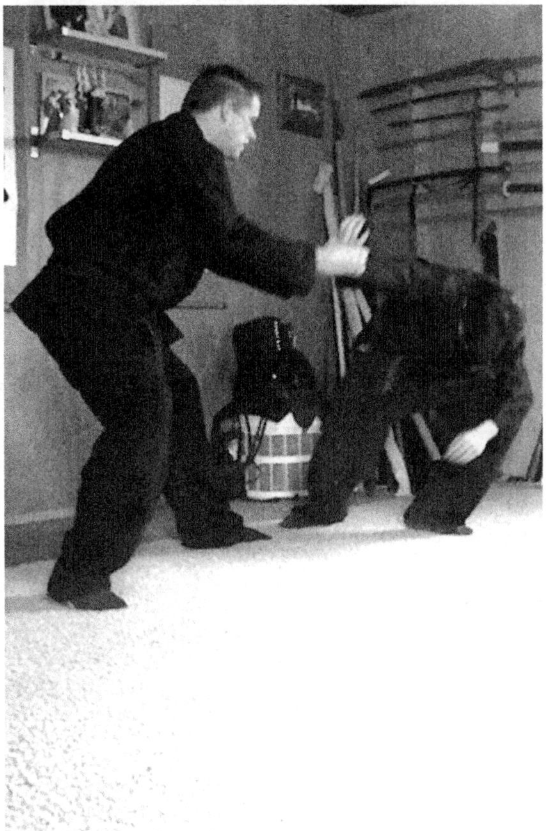

NINJUTSU: ENDURING LEGACY

Muso Dori

Unparalleled Capture

4.

相手方は左手で我が右手袖口を捕る。右手を体と共に右へ引くこと。充分大きく上より巻き込み, 逆腕を締めると同時に右足膝関節を蹴り, 敵を投げる。左技のこと。

The adversary uses his left hand to seize my right sleeve. Draw back the right hand with the body to the right. Wrap up the arm with a sufficiently big motion so that the reversed arm is wrenched and at the same time kick the knee joint so the enemy is thrown. The technique is the same on the left.

Tori and *Uke* face each other in *Shizen no Kamae*. *Uke* steps forward and seizes *Tori's* right sleeve with his left hand near the elbow. This might be done to prevent someone from freely drawing a weapon like a sword or dagger. *Tori* steps back and to the right and slides his right palm under the bony protuberance on *Uke's* right elbow. *Tori* shifts his weight to his left leg in a rocking motion forward and to the left causing Uke's balance to shift to his right leg. *Tori* will then keep *Uke's* left elbow near his body and reinforce his hold on the elbow with two hands *Tori* can then kick Uke's leg drop to drop him or go down to one knee causing *Uke* to fall forward on his face.

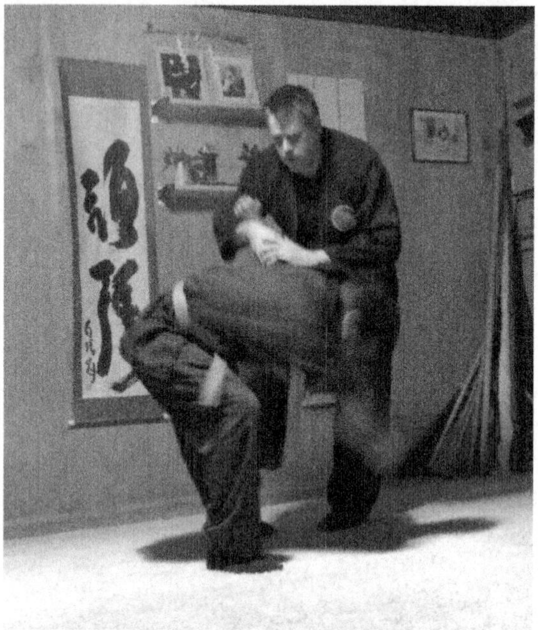

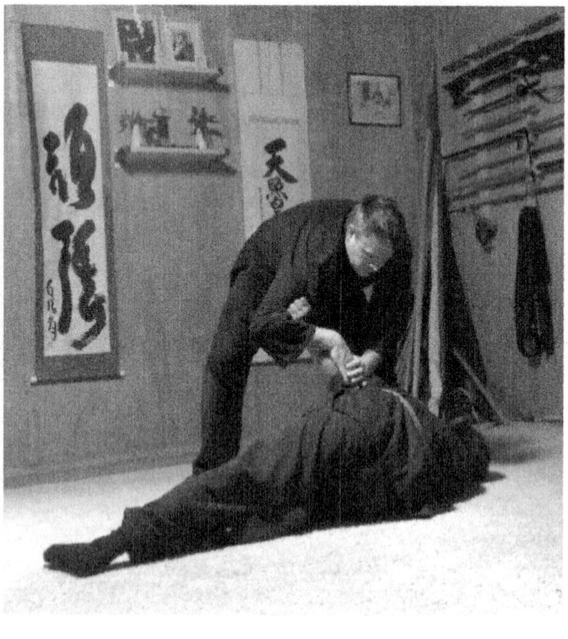

NINJUTSU: ENDURING LEGACY

From Another View

Musha Dori
Warrior Capture

5.

相手方は左手で我が右袖を捕る。右手を体と共に引き,右手を内側より敵の左腕を巻き込みで，左足を我が後方に廻し,逆投げのこと。

The adversary seizes my right sleeve with his left hand. Pull back the right hand with the body, wrap up the enemy's left hand from the inside with the right hand, turn your left leg to the rear and do a reversal throw.

     Here the *Uke* is grabbing the right sleeve instead of the left as is described above. Therefore everything is being done here on the opposite side. *Tori* and *Uke* stand facing each other in *Shizen no Kamae*. *Uke* steps forward with his left foot and seizes *Tori's* right sleeve with his left hand. *Tori* will be weary of *Uke* trying to punch with his free hand and will step out to the right with his right foot and possibly slightly back if necessary. *Tori* will keep his right hand inside of *Uke's* forearm and shift forward reaching over the top of *Uke's* left arm. *Tori* will gather up *Uke's* arm under his right armpit. *Tori* turns *Uke's* body so that his right arm cannot punch. *Tori* will clasp his hands together and kick *Uke's* leg at the knee to drop him. *Tori* maintains the hold as *Uke* falls down on his back. This technique is painful and can injure the ligaments of the elbow.

NINJUTSU: ENDURING LEGACY

NINJUTSU: ENDURING LEGACY

Another View

岩石投げ
Ganseki Nage
Throwing a Rock

Ganseki Nage is a common throw but one of the hardest to learn. It is often practiced as part of the *Kihon Happo* because it is very similar in some ways to *Muso Dori*. To begin *Tori* and *Uke* will seize each other by the lapel and sleeve in a position referred to a *kumiuchi*. *Tori* will slide step back to his rear left and this will pull *Uke* forward in that direction. As *Uke* pulls back, *Tori* can follow that motion and slide step forward with both feet to stand in front of Uke' left foot. As *Tori* moves in, he will move his right hand from the lapel to under *Uke's* left arm. Tori now steps in deep between *Uke's* legs so that his right hip is pressed against Uke's waist. At the same time *Tori* will raise both hands as if doing *Hoko no Kamae*. *Tori* will turn his hips and torso throwing *Uke* over his hip. *Uke* will be thrown forward onto his back. *Tori* must get *Uke's* weight on his right leg. If so, the throw will be easy because *Uke* will not be able to resist.

Ganseki Nage from Kumiuchi

NINJUTSU: ENDURING LEGACY

Ganseki Nage from a Right Sleeve Grab (Straight Arm)

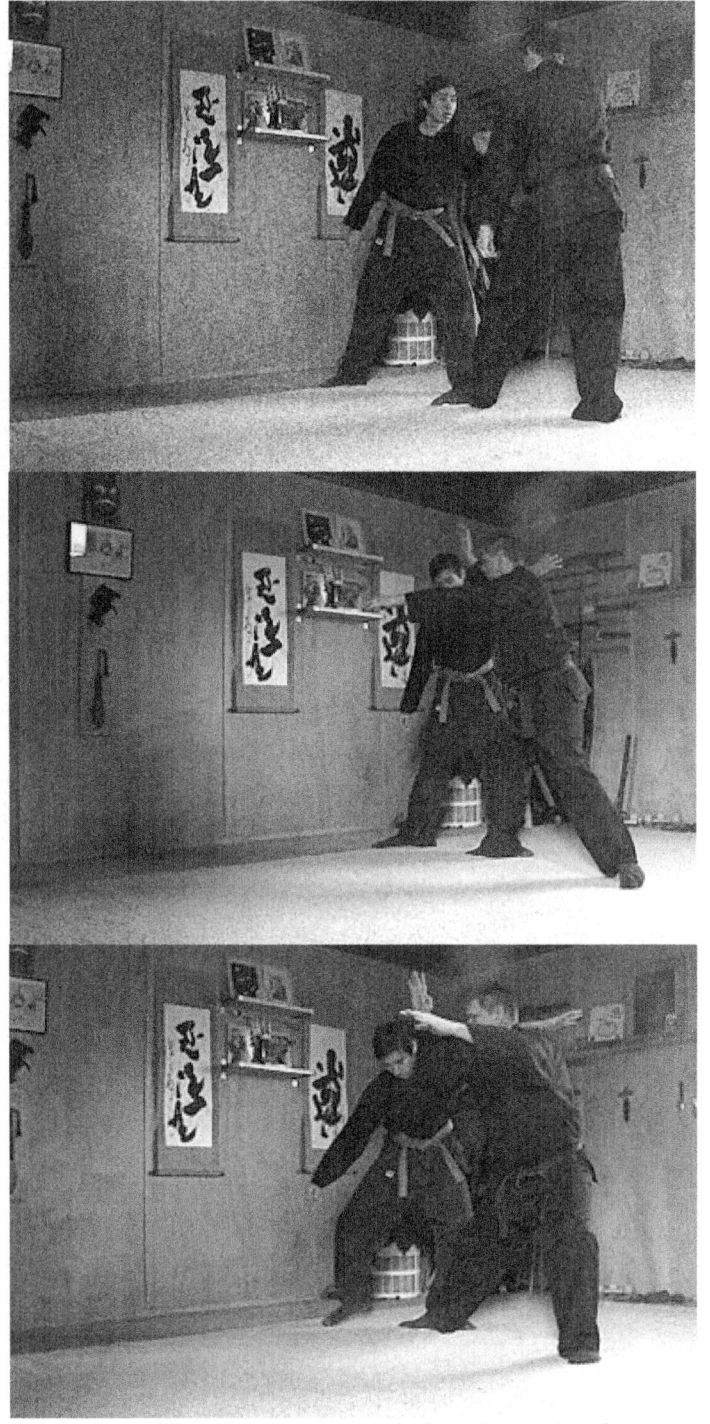

Shown here is the twisting of the hips that makes this technique project the Uke forward.

Pointers

Keep Uke's arm tight with tension as it is trapped between your neck and pressing arm.
Press with the edge of the hand or forearm against Uke's locked elbow.
Don't bend forward or his arm will slip off your neck and over your head.
Throw with a hip turn and don't use upper body strength.
Throw the Uke out and down in a spiral.
If you throw Uke in front of you he will reach you from the ground.
If you throw only outwards he may try to outrun the throw.
Your right leg in firmly placed against Uke's shin as a stumbling block.
By taking the throw Uke can release the pressure on his arm.
No fight the throw Uke's elbow will be broken.
Don't focus on the throw. Focus on potentially breaking his arm.
Go very slow and make everything fluid.
Don't rush it because it takes a long time to get this right.

Explanation of the Stiff Arm Throw

Assailants will sometimes grab the sleeve in a very tense way using strength. There bodies may be rigid and not yield easily to your movements. If someone grabs you with tension on the right sleeve, circle your right hand counterclockwise to the outside of their arm and strike down on the muscles of their forearm freeing their grip. Scoop up their stiff arm so that their wrist is at your neck and use your forearm to press their elbow joint. Turn your hips to make the throw. This variation is for the stiff person.

Explanation of the Bent Arm Ganseki Throw

If your right sleeve is grabbed and after stepping back and to the right you feel little resistance pressing your palm on the bottom side of *Uke's* elbow, you may be able to throw the *Uke* easily with a bent arm *Ganseki Nage*. This starts almost exactly the same way as *Muso Dori* except the *Uke* begins to bend his elbow so it is pointing upwards when you press it. In such cases shift your weight forward to your left leg, step in with your right leg in front of his left leg as a stumbling block, turn and throw as before with his arm bent. The picture above shows *Uke* being thrown this way. Notice that his arm is not behind the *Tori's* neck. Once you've turned to throw Uke forward you must shift first to the left leg (see picture) to pitch *Uke's* weight forward. A twist of the hips will then send him into a roll.

Ganseki Oshi-Pressing the Rock

The *Ganseki* versions we've done so far require the *Tori* to enter and and throw the *Uke*. If the *Uke* is coming at *Tori* quickly these previous variations will not work. The best thing to do is get out of the way and keep *Uke's* motion going forward. While *Uke* is coming forward his shoulders must be made different levels by raising up one of his elbows. By doing this one can get behind *Uke* so that he can be pushed forward from the rear.

Start by standing with *Uke* in *kumiuchi*. *Uke* will press your chest with his right hand that has grabbed your left lapel. Take a few steps back and then allow him to pass on your left side. At the same time, *Tori* will move his right hand up under *Uke's* left elbow and raise it up. *Tori* keeps *Uke's* right arm lower so that his shoulders don't stay level. This causes *Uke* to be thrown forward especially when you turn to the direction he is going.

Ganseki Otoshi (Dropping the Rock)

Ganseki Otoshi involves sweeping *(harai)* the *Uke's* rear leg rather rather than placing your leg against his shin. This can be done on an opponent that is strong enough to try and resist throwing or someone who just presents the opportunity. In this technique, the rear leg is swept out from under the *Uke* to he falls down like a falling rock on his face.

The opponent can either seize one sleeve or grab you in *kumiuchi*. Draw the *Uke's* balance over his front leg by stepping back and to the side and then enter to sweep his rear leg. Raise your arm(s) high under the *Uke's* arm so that we he falls he will strain his shoulder and this hold can be maintained once he falls.

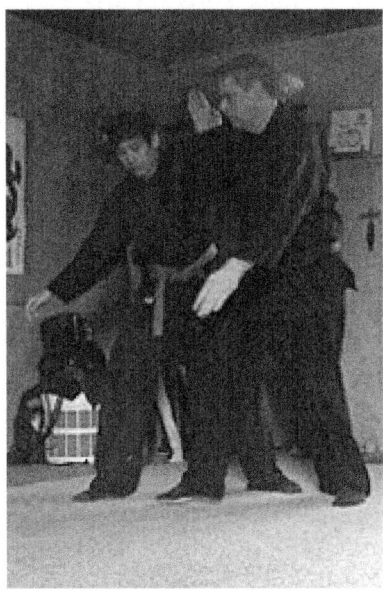

鬼砕

Oni Kudaki
Demon Crush

Oni Kudaki is a powerful technique that is often considered part of the *Kihon Happo*. It is can be done quickly and easily to break an arm. This should be done with caution. To begin, *Tori* and *Uke* face each other. *Uke* steps forward with his right foot and seizes *Tori's* left lapel with his right hand. *Tori* lifts his left hand inside of *Uke's* right forearm. *Tori* then steps forward and to the left with his left foot beyond *Uke's* right leg. At the same time *Tori* brings his right hand under *Uke's* right arm and clasps his hands together vertically as if he were clapping. Keep *Uke's* arm bent at a 90 degree angle and get his back to arch. *Tori* will now turn his hips to the left suddenly which wrenches *Uke's* right arm. This hold could injure the elbow or shoulder so be careful.

NINJUTSU: ENDURING LEGACY

Oni Kudaki against a Punch

Tori and *Uke* face each other in *Ichimonji no Kamae*. *Uke* steps forward with his right foot and attempts to punch *Tori* with his right hand. *Tori* steps back and to the right and blocks the punch with a left *Jodan Uke*. *Tori* then slide steps forward and to the left with his left foot followed by his right, and he strikes *Uke's* right shoulder with a *Fudo Ken* punch. This drives *Uke's* shoulder back and breaks his kamae. *Tori* will now step forward and take *Oni Kudaki* on *Uke's* right arm as previously described. *Tori* will extend his arms out and use the edge of his forearms to press painfully into the bones of *Uke's* arm. *Tori* then steps behind *Uke's* right leg and twists his body to throw *Uke* down.

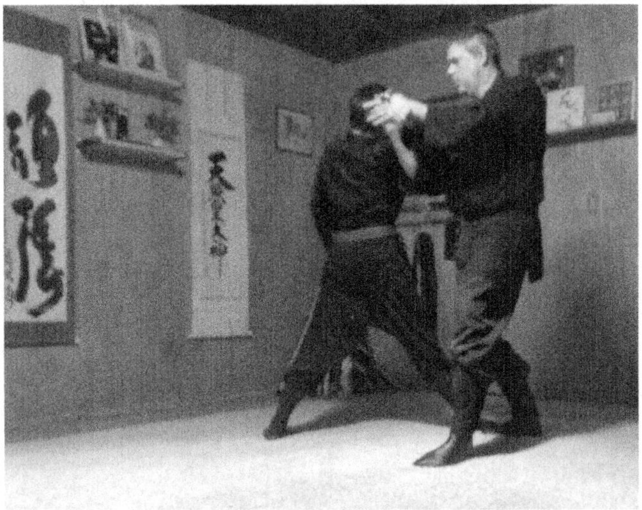

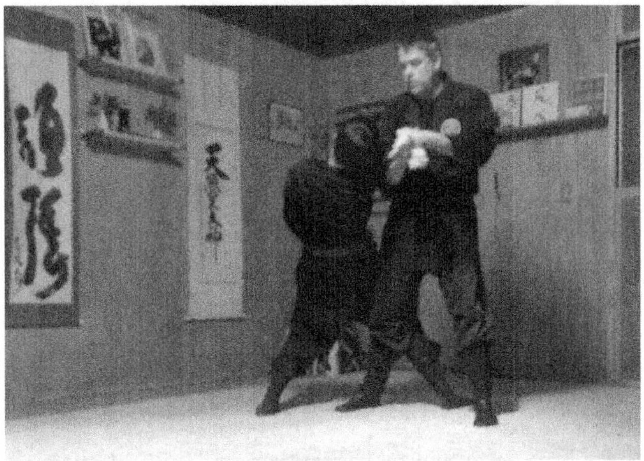

When clasping the hands together for *Oni Kudaki* and also for *Musha Dori*, put the hands together as shown in the picture. Do not lace the fingers together. The hands should be held together as though one were clapping the hands.

竹折
Take Ori
Bamboo Break

Take Ori is a powerful technique of bending the wrist at a sharp angle. The wrist naturally flexes at about a 90 degree angle. If the knuckles of the hand are pressed to make wrist bend more it causes considerable pain. To begin, *Tori* and *Uke* will face each other in *Ichimonji no Kamae*. *Tori* however will have his right foot forward. *Uke* will step forward and attempt to punch *Tori* in the face with his right fist. *Tori* intercepts the punch and guides *Uke's* balance forward to the right as the punch terminates. As *Uke* begins to pull back to regain his form, *Tori* slides his hand to *Uke's* right wrist. *Tori's* thumb and little finger form a ring around *Uke's* wrist like a bracelet. As *Uke* pulls back, his hand is followed and his wrist is compressed. *Tori* will raise the hand upwards intensifying the pain. This is also commonly used against a lapel grab.

Take Ori (Breaking Bamboo)

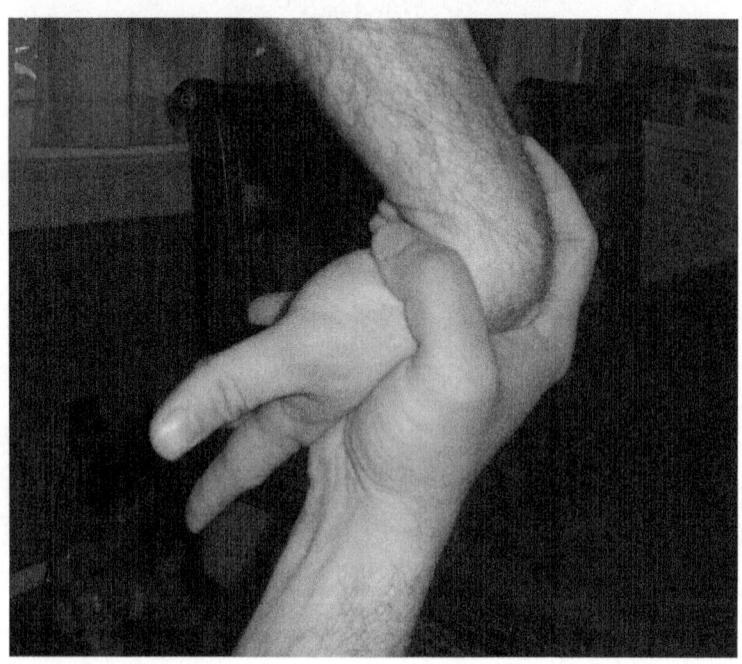

本逆
Hon Gyaku
Basic Reversal

Hon Gyaku is a painful wrist lock that is essentially a variation of *Ura Gyaku*. Please see the previous section on *Ura Gyaku*. To begin, *Tori* and *Uke* face each other in *Shizen no Kamae*. Uke steps forward and seizes *Tori's* left lapel with his right hand. Ideally, one should move enough that one is not grabbed and can intercept *Uke's* hand. *Tori* will step back and to the left with his left foot into a strong *kamae* while he seizes *Uke's* right hand with his own right hand. Tori will take *Uke's* hand off by turning his hips and applying pain with his right thumb nail to the bones of *Uke's* hands if necessary. Once the hand is off, *Tori* will move the hand up and align it with the center line of his own body. Both hands are used to bend *Uke's* hand forward. Imagine bending the wrist as if you were trying to make the pinky go towards the head. *Uke's* wrist is painfully bent sideways.

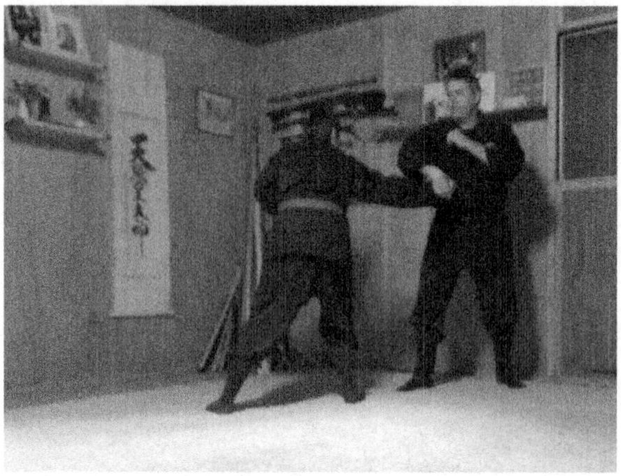

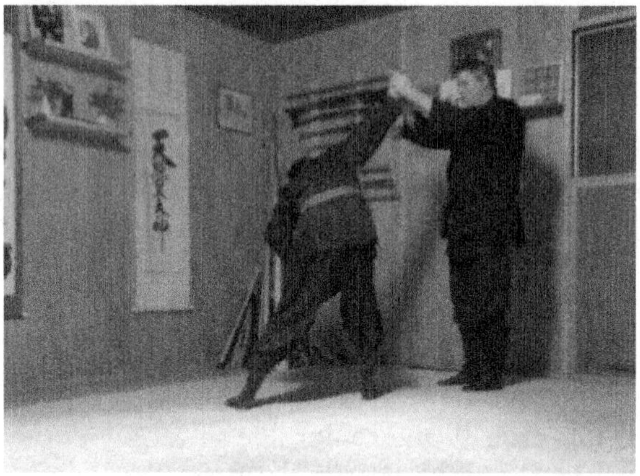

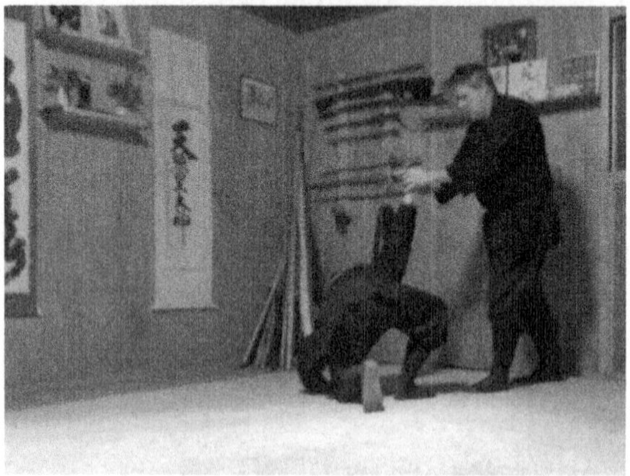

體變術無刀捕之型
Taihenjutsu Mutodori No Kata
Body Movements Unarmed Against a Sword Forms

There are three basic forms for defending yourself unarmed against a swordsman. They are *Hira no Kamae, Ichimonji no Kamae* and *Jumonji no Kamae*. As the names suggest they are taken from three postures commonly used. While practicing these forms it should be understood that they are the basics for many other variations. The strategy for these forms is to avoid being cut by evasive body movements and good timing. Practice these forms using wooden *bokken* or *shinai* for safety. Start out slowly paying careful attention to footwork and postures.

Hira no Kamae

Stand facing the swordsman in *Hira no Kamae*. The swordsman steps forward and cuts down with a straight vertical cut. Step back and to the side into *Ichimonji no Kamae* to avoid the cut. Roll away diagonally in the direction of the back leg in *Ichimonji no Kamae*. A variation is to step to the side in *Ichimonji no Kamae* rather than also stepping back. In this case, one would do a side roll rather than a diagonal roll. Techniques are about distance, angles and timing.

Ichimonji no Kamae

Stand facing the swordsman in a right *Ichimonji no Kamae*. The swordsman steps forward and cuts down with a straight vertical cut. Roll diagonally forward and to the right. The swordsman turns to the left to do another diagonal cut. As he cuts, you will rise to one knee from the roll and strike into his body at *Suigetsu* with a *Shitoken* strike. Follow up as needed by controlling the weapon and taking out the attacker with other strikes or joint locks.

Jumonji no Kamae

Stand facing the swordsman in *Jumonji no Kamae*. The swordsman steps forward and makes a vertical cut with his sword. Step back and to the side enough to avoid the cut. Then step in quickly to the right side of the swordsman and strike his neck with an *Omote Shuto*. You may also strike to his wrist or collar bone with this *Shuto* strike.

秘拳十六法
Hiken Juruppo
Sixteen Secret Fists

The *Hiken Juruppo* represent the hand and foot arsenal of the nine lineages. The word for fist here does not simply mean a closed hand for striking. The meaning is much broader. It is about making the parts of the body weapons. So weapons can be found from head to toe literally. These methods were originally brought from China to Japan probably during the late *T'ang* Dynasty which would be about the 10th Century AD. *Gyokko Ryu Kosshijutsu*, the oldest of the nine lineages of the *Bujinkan*, entered Japan around this time. The Chinese considered how best to strike different regions of the body to cause the most damage. This knowledge led to the development of ways to use the hands and feet and also a more detailed understanding of how to affect human anatomy and physiology.

For instance, when we strike *Butsumetsu* (an area from the nipple to under the armpit), the ribs could be broken, but also less muscle is protecting this area and it has a wealth of nerve endings. In addition, lymph nodes dot this area, and when hit, the lymph nodes discharge their waste back into the bloodstream. Another example is a point on both sides of the neck called *Uko or Amado*. These points are hit with *Kiten Ken*. They could cause serious injury or even death. Obviously there is a risk of breaking bones but with that aside, these points are over the Vagus Nerve which goes to the heart, carotid arteries (which bring blood to the brain) and baroreceptors that regulate blood flow to the brain. Hitting these points could cause unconsciousness. It is therefore recommended that one practice these strikes with little power when training on another individual. At the time this type of knowledge was cutting edge. Just knowing how to hit these points was not enough. After all, an enemy does not stand still. Therefore, correct distancing and angling become important so that one could actually use these types of strikes.

Below is a list of the Sixteen Fists.

鬼角拳
Kikaku Ken (Demon Head Fist)
手起拳
Shuki Ken (Elbow Fist)
不動拳
Fudo Ken (Unwavering Fist)
起転拳
Kiten Ken (Turning Fist)
指針拳
Shishin Ken (Pointer Fist)
指端拳
Shitan Ken (Fingertip Fist)
蝦蛄拳
Shako Ken (Claw Fist)
指刀拳
Shito Ken (Finger Sword Fist)
指環拳
Shikan Ken (Knuckle Ring Fist)
骨法拳
Koppo Ken (Bone Breaking Fist)
八葉拳
Happa Ken (Eight Leaf Fist)
足躍拳
Sokuyaku Ken (Foot Skip Kick)
足起拳
Sokki Ken (Knee Kick)
足逆拳
Sokugyaku Ken (Foot Reversed Fist)
体拳
Tai Ken (Body Fist)
心拳
Shin Ken (Spirit Fist)

Applications of Hiken Juruppo

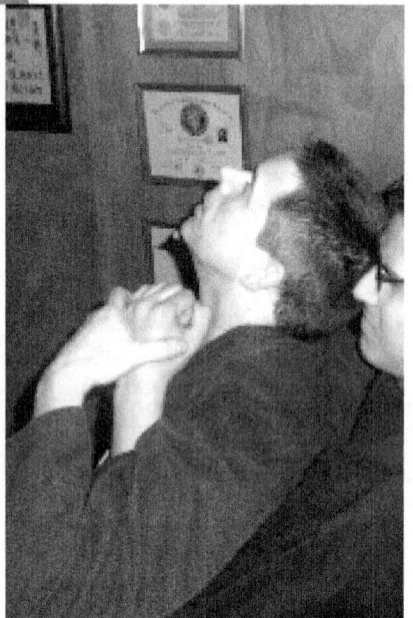

Kikaku Ken

When someone grabs you with both hands, position your body at an incline and drive the top of the forehead into their face. If grabbed from behind use the back of your head to strike the opponent's face.

Shuki Ken

At close range the elbows can strike from all directions.

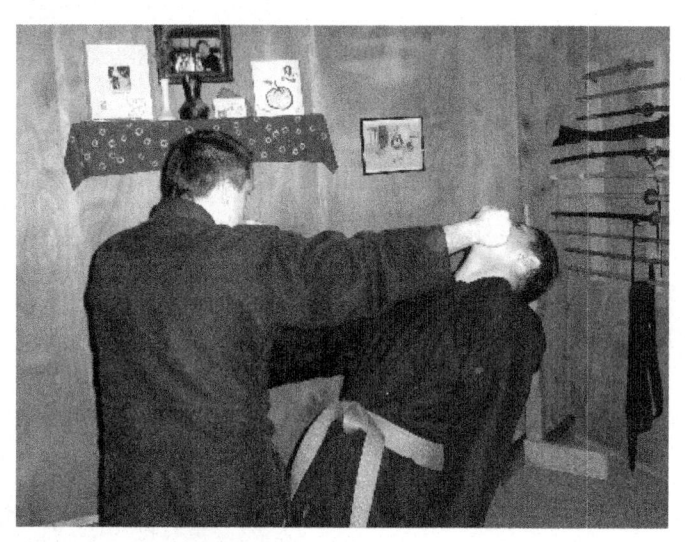

Fudo Ken

Drive through you target with a Fudo Ken until your opponent falls.

Kiten Ken

With the palm up as shown here, strike to the neck. This is called an Ura Shuto. With the palm turned up the strike is called Omote Shuto.

Shito Ken

One of the most common applications of Shito Ken is to strike into the armpit at a point called Butsumetsu. Rock into the point by shifting your weight.

NINJUTSU: ENDURING LEGACY

Shako Ken

Strike the chin with the palm and grip the face with nails. Shove the head back or rake the fingers down face.

Shako Ken

When grabbed by the lapels, take a handful of flesh at the opponent's sides or around the the back. Clench the flesh, and then shake violently.

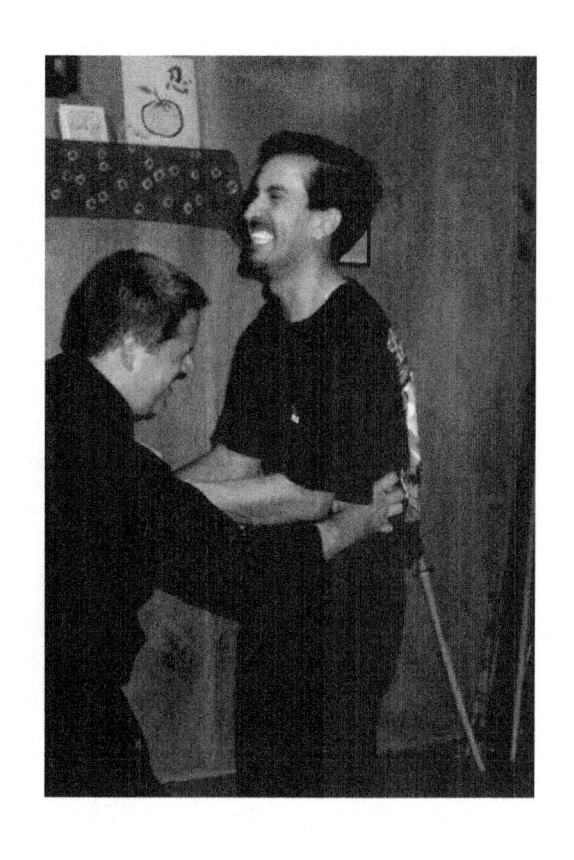

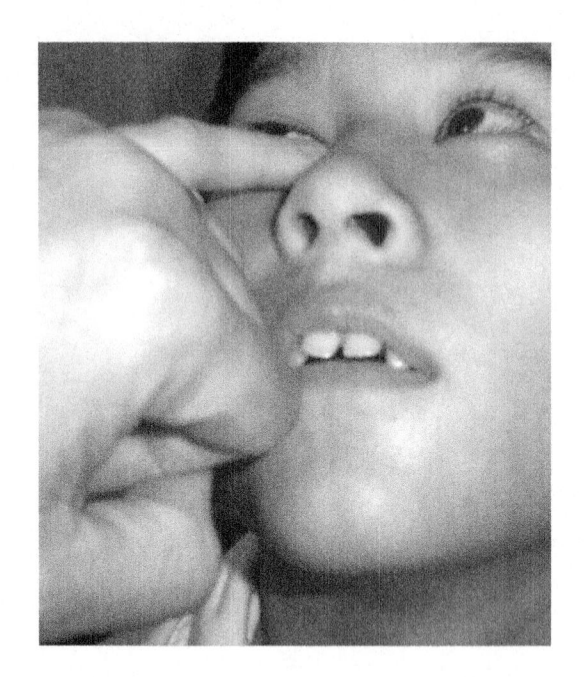

NINJUTSU: ENDURING LEGACY

Shishin Ken

The needle fist naturally finds the most sensitive areas during techniques and painfully exploits them.

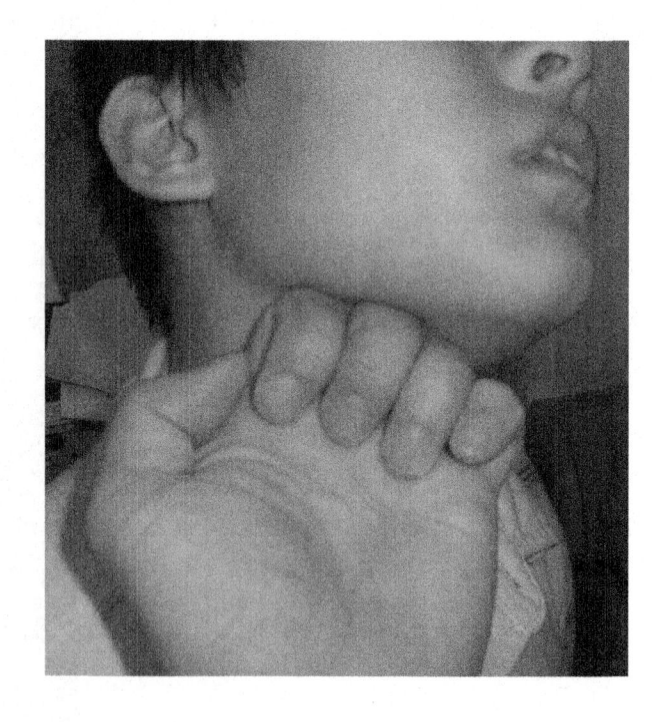

Shikan Ken

The folded knuckles concentrate the power of a strike. A hit like this could easily break the jaw.

143

NINJUTSU: ENDURING LEGACY

Sokki Ken

Use the knees to strike the groin at close distance or drop on the ribs or even the face as sown here.

Happa Ken

When grabbed with both hands, free yourself by smacking the opponent's ears with cupped hands.

Sokuyaku Ken

Suddenly strike with the heel or sole to the midpoint along the outer thigh (Soto Sai) or the inner thigh (Uchi Sai). This will cause the opponent to be unable to walk. Hook down with the kick for Soto Sai and Kick outwards for Uchi Sai. The heel is best for hitting the points.

Yoko Geri

This is how a side kick is done. Turn the hips and kick forward with the heel or sole of the foot.

破術九法
Hajutsu Kuho
Nine Methods of the Art of Destruction

There are many differences that separate *Budo Taijutsu* from other martial arts but one distinct difference that is obvious is presented here. *Budo Taijutsu* typically has its arsenal of techniques and measures to destroy the attacker's arm or leg or whatever else is being used to attack you. There are other ways to handle punches and kicks but for *Hajutsu Kuho* the focus is on overpowering the opponent. This is not done by strength or power necessarily. Often weak areas are exploited. It is almost certainly done by surprise and with intent to immediately stop an attacker's advance.

By some standards *Hajutsu Kuho* could be considered "dirty fighting." If somebody kicks you, you break the bones in their foot. If somebody punches you, you break the bones in their hands and then he can't attack you again. If you are grabbed you take a finger and bend it to the breaking point. This is the essence of *Hajutsu Kuho*. By learning these techniques well you will have a solid background in personal protection. *Hajutsu Kuho* has balance between techniques that "crush and kill" and those that free one from capture with little effort or force. *Hajutsu Kuho* reflects *Dakentaijutsu* (Striking) and *Jutaijutsu* (Grappling) aspects of *Budo Taijutsu* as well as aspects of *Kosshi Jutsu* (Soft Tissue Attack), and *Koppojutsu* (Bone Attacks).

手解
Tehodoki
Untying the Hands

When someone seizes a person's wrist it is done for control. The person may not just be trying to prevent you from moving. You might be trying to hold on to something of value or taking out something to defend yourself. If a person is close enough to grab you, then that person is close enough to hit you and vice versa. Therefore, a simple solution to being grabbed is to end the matter by striking the aggressor. The legal appropriateness of your response may dictate that you apply a less aggressive solution.

There is a tendency for most people to tense up and try to resist when they are grabbed. However, this is not necessarily the appropriate response. Although the hand may have been grabbed, the body remains free. Sometimes by taking someone's hand, the attacker intends to take their body and mind, too. A hand that grabs could also suddenly release and strike you, so don't make the assumption that it will stay there. Techniques which involve joint locking a grabbing hand typically involve placing your other hand on the opponent's hand first in case he tries to remove it suddenly.

In order for a hand to grasp an object, the thumb must close with the fingers to form a ring. Where the thumb approximates the fingers is the weak link. Do not try to jerk the hand away. Turn or position the body and arm in a direction in which walking or moving the whole body will free the hand by allowing the hand to break through this link in the ring.

Find the right angle and right direction for movement and all of this will require very little effort. Strength comes from solid footing. If you are in motion even before you are grabbed then the opponent must move also to calibrate his musculature to your location. The strength to hold you in place will require the opponent to be static and not in motion. When you stop moving the opponent finds you and calibrates his strength based on a static position. The principle to be learned here is keep moving.

Tehodoki Gata
Hand Escaping Forms

Omote Tekubi Dori
Single Wrist Grab on the Same Side

Uchi Mawashi Dori (Turning to the Inside)

Uke grabs *Tori's* right wrist with his left hand.
Tori takes a right step in front of *Uke's* left foot.
Tori extends his fingers on his right hand and turns his hand palm down.
Tori then pivots on the right foot and turns counterclockwise (tenkan).
As *Tori* turns his right forearm may bump *Uke's* right forearm to help release *Uke's* grip.
The elbow strike or bump is a part of a continuous motion and not a separate action.
There are no pauses.
Maintain eye contact and don't turn your back to the *Uke*.
You may strike *Uke* after getting away.

Soto Mawashi Dori (Turning to the Outside)

Uke grabs *Tori's* right wrist with his left hand.
Tori takes a left step forward and out to the right as he turns his right hand palm up.
Tori's right elbow is positioned against his body and his forearm points to *Uke's* left rear quandrant.
Tori will now simply walk in the direction of *Uke's* left rear quadrant.
Tori will not try to jerk away.
Uke's hand will break free because he will not be able to maintain his grip.
You may strike *Uke* after getting away.

Yahuza Gake (Losing and Sticking)

Uke grabs *Tori's* right wrist with his left hand.
Tori steps out to the right side and takes an *Ura Gyaku* on *Uke's* left hand.
Tori then steps back with his left leg, and uses his right arm to do a smashing armbar with his forearm to *Uke's* left extended elbow.
Tori maintains a *Take Ori* on *Uke's* left wrist.
Tori drops his weight through the elbow joint.
Disturb *Uke's* balance by getting his weight more on one leg when bringing the *Ura Gyaku* from a 6:00 position to a 12:00 position.
Do not allow *Uke* to maintain a solid fixed kamae even if he is bent over at the waist from the smashing arm bar.
Use the counterclockwise turn of the hips to power the arm break.

Ura Tekubi Dori
Single Cross Grab

Kakae Hiji Dori (Sticking to the Elbow Capture)

Uke grabs *Tori's* right wrist with his right hand.
Tori takes a short step back and to the right to turn *Uke's* shoulders and arm.
Tori now faces to the right perpendicular to *Uke's* stance.
Tori steps forward with his left foot hitting just above the elbow with his upper arm near the shoulder.
This either breaks *Uke's* extended right arm at the elbow or causes him to go into a projection throw.

Uchi Mawashi Hazushi (Turning to the Inside and Crushing)

Uke grabs *Tori's* right wrist with his right hand.
Tori steps to the outside of the grab (left) with his left foot and rotates his right hand around the outside of *Uke's* right grabbing hand as if to take *Ura Gyaku*.
Tori then turns his hips clockwise to the right and smashes *Uke's* extended right arm at the elbow with his forearm to break it.
Make sure *Uke's* arm is straight when you apply the break.
It should be in full extension.
Break the elbow from the outside to inside with hip torque.

Variation:
Use the thumb and index finger to form an iron horseshoe shape that rises up to grip *Uke's* right hand. This is done with *Tori's* right hand from the cross grab. This is basically an *Ura Take Ori*. *Tori* then takes a left step and uses his palms to pancake the hand into an *Ura Gyaku*. *Tori* can finish in a variety of ways.

Itami Kazushi (Crushing Pain)

Uke grabs *Tori's* right wrist with his right hand.
Tori steps out to the left and makes a small circle over *Uke's* grabbing hand counterclockwise from inside to outside.
As *Tori* circles his hand around *Uke's* hand, *Tori's* right thumb is positioned on the inner part of *Uke's* wrist at a point located on the inner wrist over the median nerve. *Tori* steps back with his right leg and reinforces the hold on the wrist point with his left hand. *Tori* presses down into the painful point with pressure from both thumbs dropping *Uke* to the ground.

Ryote Tekubi Dori
2 Hands Grab 1 Wrist

Soto Mawashi Dori (Outer Turn Capture)

Uke grabs the right wrist with both hands. Step forward and to the side of the lower grabbing hand. Rotate your own hand in a circular manner around to the outside of *Uke's* hand and then over it. Shift your weight to the forward leg as you do this and turn your hip to the left. Now turn to the right using your hip and shift your weight to what was your rear foot. This will turn his arm over so the elbow is up. Apply an armbar to *Uke's* right arm.

Keep *Uke's* hand close to your chest and try getting *Take Ori* on *Uke's* wrist.

Uchi Mawashi Dori (Inner Turn Capture)

This is similar to the technique above except *Tori* will make a circular motion of the hand to the inside of *Uke's* right forearm instead of the outside. Apply the armbar to *Uke's* left hand and not the right.

Naka Hiki (Center Pull)

Grab your own right palm with your left hand. Don't interlace the fingers. Step back with your left foot and rock back to your rear foot. As you rock back break his grip with a whole body motion. The hands become free and continue the motion with an *Ura Shuto* strike done vertically to the face with the right hand.

Uchi Mawashi Dori-Turning to the Inside

Ryote Kubi Ryote Dori
2 Hands Grab Both Wrists

Sayu Mawashi Dori (Left and Right Turn Capture)

The *Uke* grabs both hands from the front. Turn the palms of both hands up and step forward with your right foot to the outside of the *Uke's* left leg. Pivot and turn to the left so that you are facing the same direction as your partner. As you turn, his arms will cross each other and weaken his hold on you. You may gather his arms with your right arm and step forward to throw him or apply leverage under one or both of his arms at the elbow with your right shoulder.

Ogami Dori (Great Spirit Capture)

Raise your hands up out to the sides but a little in front of you. Get *Uke's* energy and balance to rise. Clap your hands together where his face is to shock *Uke* and get his head back. With the hands together in as if praying, thrust into his throat with the fingers having the palms together.

Shuko Uchi Ate Dori (Striking with Knucles of the Hand Capture)

Uke grabs both of *Tori's* wrists from the front. *Tori* then takes a right over left cross step and at the same time, lifts his right hand up slightly in a fist. Turn the right wrist so that the back of *Uke's* hand is facing down. Strike the back of *Uke's* left hand onto the protruding knuckle sticking up on his right hand One is basically striking *Uke's* hand against his own hand.

Kata Dogi Dori
Grabbing the Clothes with One Hand

Hiji Gyaku Dori (Locking the Elbow Capture)
Uke grabs *Tori's* right sleeve. Take a left step straight back and place the left palm on the bottom of *Uke's* right elbow. This traps *Uke's* arm in the bend of *Uke's* right elbow. This is *Muso Dori*.

Hoshi Jime (Wrenching the Elbow Point)
Uke grabs *Tori's* right sleeve. *Tori* grabs *Hoshi (nerve over funny bone)* with his left hand and raises *Uke's* left arm. *Tori* takes *Omote* or *Ura Gyaku* and throws *Uke*.

体解

Taihodoki
Untying the Body

Taihodoki includes ways in which the body can escape from being grabbed. In this category we are dealing with bearhugs from both the front and back. A bearhug is used to squeeze the air out of someone, to injure the ribs or a way to control a person before slamming them to the ground. These bearhugs can be done over the arms or under the arms.

Obviously if the attacker grabs over the arms this will limit the ability to use your arms for defense, but it also limits the attacker's ability to successfully squeeze the air out of you. By grabbing under the arms the attacker is leaving himself wide open to be struck in the face with the elbows if the person that is grabbed suddenly turns. By grabbing with both hands, the attacker has to commit himself and his hands are not free to do other things like striking.

Bearhugs over the Arms from the Front

When grabbed in this way, I recommend the following:
1. Keep a wide solid base with your feet to avoid being thrown.
2. Make yourself bigger at the moment of being grabbed by bringing your arms away from your sides. In this way the attacker may not be able to get his arms around you.
3. Expand your chest as this will also help your torso to have a larger circumference.
4. Be careful of being hit by the attacker's head and use your own head to strike his face.
5. Raise the knee up into the groin.
6. Stomp your heel into the foot and grind.
7. Grab the flesh on the sides of the waist with both hands. Squeeze and then shake the flesh violently.
8. Grab the flesh on the inside of the thigh or seize the testicles, squeeze and shake them violently.
9. Use both thumbs to press into *Koi* (a point located between the groin and hip on the inguinal ligament.

Bearhugs under the Arms from the Front

1. Cup both palms and slap the ears.
2. Sharply strike both kidneys with the edge of the hands.
3. Use the index and middle fingers to press into *murasame* (the sternal notch where there is access to the windpipe).
4. Seize the face with both hands and drive the thumbs into both eyes.
5. Seize the hair at the back of the head with both hands and pull down.
6. Strike the chin with the palm, drive the head back and down causing the attacker to lose balance and fall.
7. Grab the face with both hands so that the fingers did into flesh just below the jaw line and the index fingers dig into the eyes.
8. Grab the hair on the back of the head with one hand and the chin with the palm of the other hand. Twist the attacker's head until he falls down.
9. Strike into the neck with a *Shuto* or smash the nose with a *Shako Ken*.

Bearhug from Behind over the Arms

1. Breathe in making your chest bigger. Breathe out and slip through the opponent's grasp.
2. Use the back of your head to strike the attacker's face.
3. Stomp the opponent's feet.
4. Step forward and throw the opponent over your right hip like a horse throwing a rider.
5. Turn your body sideways so that opponent will have difficulty getting his arms around you.

Bearhug from Behind under the Arms

1. Swing the elbows to strike the opponent's face.
2. Seize a finger and twist it for control in the opponent laces his fingers.
3. Bend over and pick up the attacker's leg or legs to make him fall backwards.
4. Strike the testicles by kicking up between the attacker's legs or crushing them with the hand.
5. Step behind one of his legs, bend down and pick up the opponent by both legs and throw him down.

Bearhugs over the arms do not completely immobilize the defenders arms. Many people freeze and panic in a futile struggle. When grabbed examine where the grab is. Not by a long thought process but by a momentary sensory assessment of the situation. The grab must occur above or below the elbow. If below the elbow, the elbows can be used to wiggle out because there is leverage. If above the elbow, the elbows can bend allowing one to move one's hands and forearms. Bearhugs by nature put the attacker very close and generally a person will have to put his head to either side of your own to grab this close. If the person does not move his head to one side, the head strike is there for the taking.

If one senses that one is being grabbed from behind in a bearhug, one should make the body bigger. By this I mean inhale and fill the lungs with air. Bring the arms out slightly away from the body. The target the attacker grabs will be larger in circumference and may be impossible to get arms around. Once the attacker is on, one has space to slip out by relaxing the body and becoming small by comparison.

The headbutt may be enough to cause the attacker to let go. Lowering one's center is also important, and this is achieved by stepping out to the side and bending one's knees. By lowering your center, it will be harder for an attacker to try to throw you. The slamming back of the hips may be enough to send the attacker flying back behind you. If not proceed with the technique as described. The headbutt and the slamming of the hips distract the attacker and weaken his resolve to maintain a solid hold.

When lifting the arms up, do so vigorously and unexpectedly. A failed attempt will cause the attacker to become wise to this type of escape. Once the arms are up, take the *Ganseki Otoshi* (like *Ganseki Nage*, but drop Uke straight down). One can slide the left leg back into the attacker's right leg or slam into it. It really depends on the strength and *kamae* of the attacker. Once the opponent is down, do not let go of your hold on his arm. His right arm is naturally bent back and one can immobilize him easily from this position. As before, immobilize the opponent or stomp his face. Maintain *Zanshin* (mindfulness).

Strangle Hold From the Rear

Tori stands in *Shizen no Kamae*. *Uke* walks up from behind and chokes *Tori* in a *Sangyaku Jime* (Triangular Choke which is about the same as a Sleeper Hold). As soon as anything starts coming around the neck, raise the shoulders up as if you were shrugging them. This is essentially another way of making yourself bigger. The effect is like a turtle going into its shell. Immediately, grab into the enemy's right *hoshi* point on his elbow's medial epicondyle on the arm attempting to grab you with your right hand. Seize his right hand hand with your left hand. Now slip under the arm and swiftly bring your left leg back so that it sweep his right leg out from under him and he falls to the ground.

The word *miyaku* means to strangle. The artery in this technique is definitely the carotid artery. It should be noted that at the level of the Adam's Apple and on either side are the carotid arteries and baroreceptors. Baroreceptors sense changes in pressure namely blood pressure. By choking around the neck the supply of oxygen in diminished to the brain and the person may feint and need to be revived. Pressure on the baroreceptors can also cause a person to feint.

To choke a person from behind I have found that the person is immediately alerted to someone putting their right arm for example around the neck. I have found that tapping the left shoulder first guides the person's attention to the left shoulder and one can slip the right forearm snuggly against the throat from the person's right side. As the person's attention switches from the left shoulder to their throat their head turns into the choking forearm. This should be practiced with caution because on could injure the Adam's Apple.

If being choked by the means described above it is likely that the attacker is going to try to get *Sangyaku Jime* or Triangular Choke. To do this he will get his right hand in contact with his left upper sleeve or shoulder and put his left hand behind your head making a solid lock. This is tougher to get out of and one should obviously avoid this position. As one senses that the attacker's right arm is going around your neck, use your left hand to catch his right forearm to prevent him from getting a solid lock around your neck. Turn your to the right so that your feet are as they would be a right foot forward *Ichimonji no Kamae*. If the hold is not tight and you have caught his right forearm with your left hand, arch your neck back and deliver a smash to his face with the back of your head. This may be done once or even repeated if he attempts to dodge it. Lower your hips and even step out to the side if necessary. Use your right thumbnail of your right hand to dig into the *hoshi kyusho* point around the medial epicondyle of his right humerus. Also, use the nails of your left hand to dig into the back of his right hand as you put an *Omote Gyaku* type reversal on it. Throw the opponent over your right hip and then stomp into his right side.

Sankaku Jime or Triangular Choke

Full Nelson Hold

Uke comes from behind *Tori* and grabs him under the arms in a Half Nelson. In other words, *Uke* is using both his forearms to pull back on *Tori's* arms with the intent of clasping his hands together behind *Tori's* head. When this happens, *Tori* should immediately get a strong and wide base and slams both of his elbows down abruptly to break *Uke's* grip and sandwich *Uke's* arms at the sides of the body. *Tori* will reach up and seize *Uke's* fingers as if he were climbing a ladder. *Tori* then brings both of *Uke's* arms out to the sides and then around again if front of his body. This twists all of *Uke's* fingers painfully. *Tori* can now control or throw *Uke*. Although both hands are captured by the fingers, *Tori* can concern himself by throwing *Uke* only using one hand.

親殺子殺
Oyagoroshi and Kogoroshi
Killing the Thumb and Little Finger

When an attacker grabs the lapel one can either do *Oyagoshi* or *Kogoroshi* easily depending on how one is grabbed. Strangely, the Japanese call the thumb the parent and the little finger the child. So, the name is written as "killing the parent" and "killing the child." Both are examples of punishing the fingers by twisting them, cutting them with the fingernails, or pressing painfully into the cuticles to cause pain. Other fingers besides these could be used. In addition, weapons could be used to inflict pain on the fingers to control an opponent.

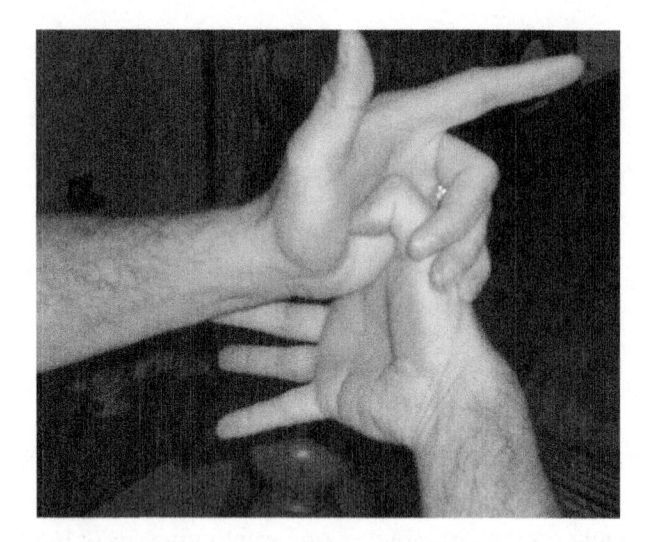

Oyagoroshi

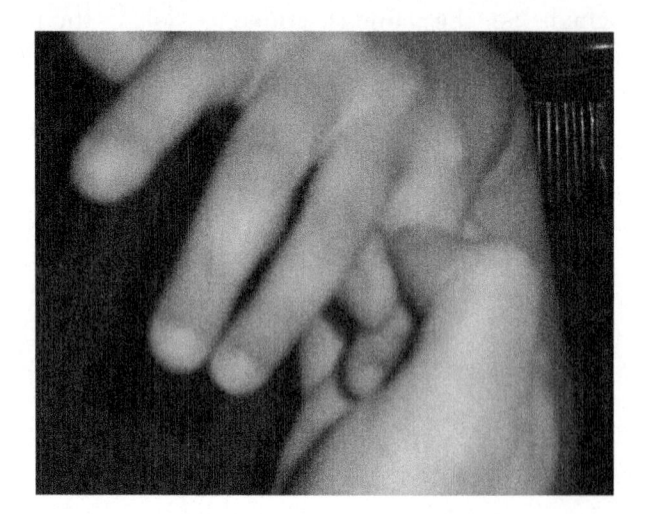

Kogoroshi

Kogoroshi

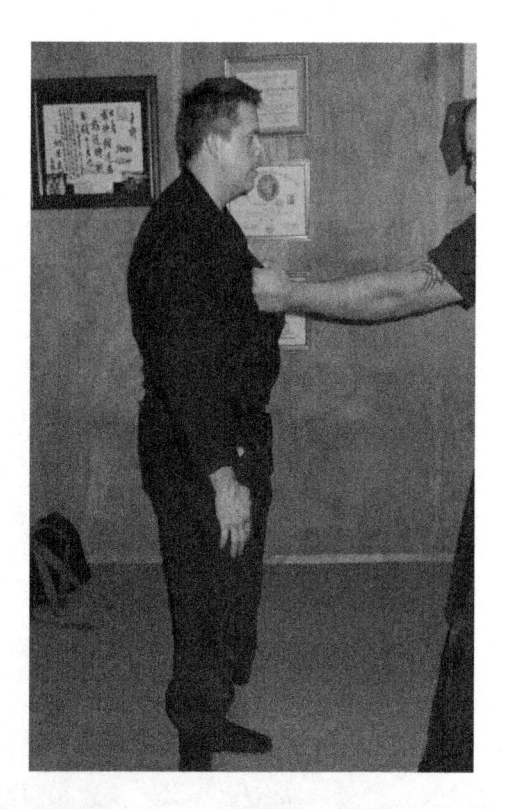

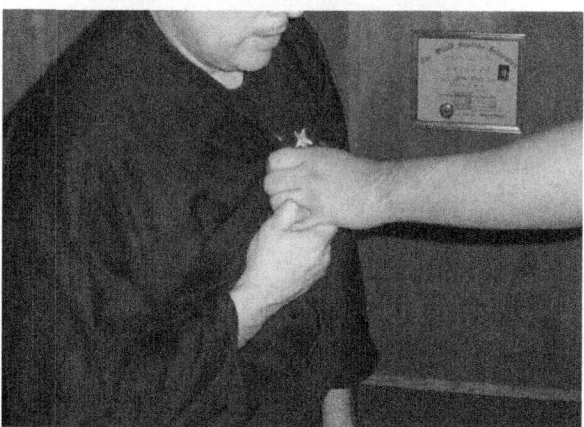

When the chest is seized by the left hand, step back with the right foot and slide your thumb down the back of the *Uke's* hand to probe between the webbing of the fingers. Drive your nail into this sensitive tissue. This causes a sharp, stabbing pain that will cause the *Uke* to want to immediately let go.

Oyagoroshi

If the attacker seizes the lapel with the left hand, step back with the left foot, and place your left palm at the tip of his left thumb. Push up to bend his thumb with the palm and use the tips of your left finger to compress the joint of the thumb. This will not only cause pain in the joints of the knuckle but also cause pain in the nail.

腰砕

Koshi Kudaki
Crushing the Hips

Koshi Kudaki is commonly done when someone attempts to throw you with a *Judo* style throw. The throw could be *Koshi Nage* (hip throw), or *Seoi Nage* (back-bearing throw) for example. As *Uke* turns his back to throw with his hips, one can step back with one leg to stabilize and attack the *Uke*'s hips. *Koshi* can mean back, hips, waist or pelvis. This general area all fits into the category of "*koshi*." Using different body parts can be effective in attacking the opponent's hips. I will give some examples to start exploring the principle of attacking the hips.

Using the Hands

1. As *Uke* steps into a right hip throw with his back turned, *Tori* will step back with his right leg and strike *Uke* just above the right ilium with the side of his left hand and wrist using a *Shuto* or *Shito Ken*. This point that one strikes is called *Shichibatsu* which means "seven days." Apparently, this is about how long it takes to heal if you hit it correctly. The point is just above the center of the iliac crest on each side.

2. As *Uke* steps in for a right hip throw with his back turned, *Tori* steps back with his left leg and strikes *Uke* just above the right ilium with the side of his right hand and wrist using a *Shuto*.

3. As *Uke* steps in for a right hip throw with his back turned, *Tori* will block and strike at the same time into the right side of *Uke's* pelvis with the arms crossed as in *Jumonji no Kamae* hitting *Uke* with two *Fudo Ken*.

4. As *Uke* steps in for a right hip throw with his back turned, *Tori* will step back with his right leg and keep his back erect. *Tori* draws his right shoulder back, and drives a left *Boshiken* into the point at the top of ilium. A *Boshiken* may also used to strike just above the bony prominence that one can feel at the side of the hip. Drive into this point and the opponent will fall down.

5. As *Uke* steps into a right hip throw with his back turned, *Tori* steps back and strikes as example 2 and then uses his left knee to strike into the back of the pelvis.

Dealing with Spinning Kicks

Some styles will use techniques that expose the back while punching or kicking. For example, spinning backfists and spinning heel kicks that require that the kicker turn away from his opponent for a moment in motion. It is at this moment that a front stomp kick can be applied to the pelvis. At the right distance, the points mentioned earlier could be kicked with the heel. The knees may also be used if the distance is closer.

Using the Hips

Slamming the hips into the *Uke's* hips can cause him to lose balance and can potentially injure his hips. One can do this as *Uke* is punching, kicking or attempting to throw you.

The Limits of the Pelvis

Flexibility varies from person to person. At some point if the knees are opened too far apart this will cause extreme pain and possible injury to the pelvis and some of the surrounding muscles. This principle is particularly useful when dealing with someone who kicks. When the legs are crossed a strike from side to side horizontally through the pelvis can be very effective in disturbing the balance. Also, if one sweeps an opponent's leg out from under him, at times his legs will be painfully straddled and injure the pelvis.

蹴砕

Keri Kudaki
Crushing Kicks

Keri Kudaki involves crushing the opponent's kicks by various means. If the opponent kicks, and his leg is injured in the process, he will not try to kick again or he may very well be unable to stand. As a general rule, hard targets such as the knees are not struck directly with a crushing strike. The danger of course is that one injures oneself in the process. Hard targets that make up joints such as the hip, knee and ankle are attacked by strikes or joint locks that cause these joint to twist and therefore rupture. This can be done by using angles of attack that compromise the joint. For instance, to create lateral instability in the knee, one presses the joint from the inside. To create medial instability of the knee joint one would press from the outside. A technique like *Jigoku Otoshi* uses this principle. In *Jigoku Otoshi*, one captures the opponent's right front kick with the right hand from the outside and then brings the left knee down on the opponent's knee joint to press down. This drops the opponent immediately. Not dropping soon enough results in serious injury to the knee.

When attacking muscles, a direct, hard attack is delivered to paralyze the leg and flog large muscle groups. This is the case when striking the thigh. There are two main points located on the thigh that are good for striking. They are *Uchi Sai* (midpoint of inner thigh) and *Soto Sai* (midpoint of outer thigh.) If the opponent attacks with a right *Zenpo Geri* (Front Kick), step forward and to the right to get inside the leg. Then, strike with a right *Fudo Ken* to *Uchi Sai* on the attacker's right leg thigh. One can also step forward and to the left and strike *Soto Sai* with a left *Fudo Ken*.

Striking the calf either from the inside or outside the kick is also an option. As the opponent attacks with a *Zenpo Geri*, step forward and to the side to get off line and strike his *Kobura* (Calf) with a *Gedan Uke* blocking strike. This kind of block can be done as one is moving forward or even walking by the kick. Besides striking the calf one can also strike *Soto Sai*. One may also side step forward and to the side by cross stepping (*yoko aruki*) and kicking up under the calf, thigh or even into the groin as someone attempts to kick with a Front Kick.

NINJUTSU: ENDURING LEGACY

Keri Kudaki

拳砕
Ken Kudaki
Crushing Fists

When an opponent attacks with a punch, strike his arm so that he will not be able to punch again. Striking upwards into the bones of the elbow with the fist can also be very effective. This takes a bit more accuracy but this comes with practice.

Striking the inner forearm with the fist is probably one of the most common ways of blocking that we use. The hand makes a circular motion before hitting the arm to block. This motion is not independent of the whole body. In fact, the hips and shoulders should all be integrated so that a powerful block can be applied which is strong from the ground up. The arm really only appears to make a circular block. It is really the motion of the hips and shoulders that cause this movement. The point of this block is to injure the opponent's striking weapon. In this sense, it is not really a block at all.

A *Fudo Ken* fist is typically used, but a *Kiten Ken* can also be used. Destroying the opponent's punches could be done in a variety of ways. Here are some suggestions:

1. Practice strike blocking to the inside of the arm or elbow by stepping back to the right of an incoming right punch into *Ichimonji no Kamae*. Repeat this on both sides.

2. Practice strike blocking to the outside of the hand or elbow by stepping back and to the left of an incoming right punch into *Ichimonji no Kamae*. Repeat this on both sides.

3. Practice hitting the same target twice when strike/blocking to compound the pain and damage.

足砕
Toki Kudaki
Crushing Feet

Here are some examples of ways to apply *Toki Kudaki*:
1. Stomp on the top of the foot with heel and grind when you are grabbed.
2. Strike into the top of the opponent's kicking foot with your fist.
3. Use weapons like the staff to strike into the top of the opponent's feet.

八法蹴

Happo Keri
Eight Methods of Kicking

Certain kicks of the *Happo Geri* seem to be consistent from dojo to dojo. There exist some variations, however. Here are the kicks of the *Happo Geri* as I learned them.

1. Right heel kick to opponent's left inner thigh.
2. Right heel kick to opponent's left outer thigh.
3. Right toe kick to groin.
4. Right kick across to opponent's right knee or inner thigh.
5. Left heel kick to opponent's right inner thigh.
6. Left heel kick to opponent's right outer thigh.
7. Left toe kick to groin.
8. Left kick across to opponent's left knee or inner thigh.

Some dojos may use different combinations of kicks or substitutions that are different from what I have here. I have seen people throw combinations as part of the *Happo Geri*. Also, the order of the kicks may vary. Whatever the order or substitutions, the *Happo Geri* prepares one to throw devastating kicks into the opponent's legs to injure or to break his *kamae*.

It is actually more important how one throws these kicks than worrying about the right order. For instance, do not snap the kicks. These kicks are thrown through the leg. In other words, don't peck at the legs with these kicks. Once a leg is kicked, the person should not be able to stand. The foot is bent meaning that the ankle is kept flexed while kicking. When using the toes, learn to point the toes like a finger. Kicks to the groin can strike the testicles directly or may be used to thrust into the inguinal ligaments.

The effects of these various kicks, when applied to the knees, are potentially very dangerous. The knee may be kicked but the weight of the body comes forward pressing down on the leg itself until it collapses. As one leg is kicked, balance may be shifted to the other leg. When that leg is kicked the opponent will indeed have no leg no stand on.

Practice these kicks from the following situations:

1. *Tori* and *Uke* both stand apart from each in *Shizen no Kamae*. *Tori* attacks *Uke* with the *Happo Geri*.
2. *Tori* steps up to *Uke* who is standing in *Shizen* and performs one kick from the *Happo Geri*.
3. *Tori* steps up to *Uke* who is standing in *Shizen* and performs combinations from the *Happo Geri*.
4. *Tori* and *Uke* face each other in *Kumiuchi* (both *Tori* and *Uke* seize each other's lapel and sleeve) and Tori performs single kicks or combinations from the *Happo Geri*.
5. *Uke* attacks *Tori* with a punch and *Tori* responds by using the *Happo Geri*.
6. *Uke* attacks *Tori* with a *Judo* type throw and *Tori* responds using the *Happo Geri*.

Putting the Basics Together

It is essential to take the basic elements of *Taijutsu* and use them freely. This next section will show some examples of how to put together the basic elements of blocking, striking, joint locking and throwing. The examples that are shown deal with principles that illustrate ways that the *kamae* and *kihon happo* can be used. I will also take the opportunity to explain some of the underlying philosophy that is present in some of these movements.

Distance, Timing and Angles

It impossible to prepare for every type of attack that could be used against you. However, all attacks whether standing or on the ground must be done using the mechanics of the human body in space and time. Techniques are useful to learn this art, but to apply it freely one must go beyond memorization of prescribed movements and see how the underlying principles involved.

Punching Drill

This drill is designed to help develop punching skills by working on proper distance, power, angles and timing. The person holding the target has an equally important role. He is actually holding the target near the face to provide a targer for the puncher. Every time the partner punches he moves out of the way to one side and holds up the other target near his face. His job is also to learn the proper distance, timing and angles to defend against a punch.

To practice this drill the puncher will stand in a left *Ichimonji no Kamae* and punch with a right *Tsuki*. The targer holder will initially stand in *Shizen no Kamae* holding the target up, but will step of to the right in *kamae*. The target holder will then hold up the other targer in his right hand near his face to encourage a second punch. The puncher will have to turn his body to the left and cross to punch the target in this way. The target holder will step back and to the left with his left foot to get out of the way.

NINJUTSU: ENDURING LEGACY

Destroying Form

In this art the goal of a conflict is resolution which ends in your own safety. Whereas some martial arts may emphasize destroying the opponent by overwhelming him with fetal blows, our *Taijutsu* attempts to break the foundation in which the opponent is able to continue his attack. This typically means breaking his balance and getting him out of stable *kamae*.

Blocking and Disrupting Balance

Tori and *Uke* face each other in *Ichimonji no Kamae*. *Uke* steps forward with his right foot and attempts to punch *Tori* in the face with a right *Tsuki*. *Tori* steps back and to the right and raises his left fist up in *Jodan Uke* to shield himself from the punch. *Tori's* right hand comes up to counter strike. *Tori* will twist his hips to the left and strike *Uke's* right forearm with a right *Shuto* strike to destroy *Uke's* balance and structure thereby delaying his advance.

This is a very basic technique that coordinates the actions of blocking and quickly returning a strike. The sudden turn of the hips allows *Tori* to imbalance the *Uke* by using the power of the whole body to affect the *Uke's* entire core.

NINJUTSU: ENDURING LEGACY

Simplicity

It is hard to resist the temptation of doing more than is necessary. Sometimes all that is necessary is not being in the wrong place at the wrong time. Mirror the opponent's simple movements with simple movements of your own. It is the most basic of these movements that will be the most useful and practical.

Defending Against a Left Jab Using Kamae

It is necessary and essential that one be able to use the basics of this art to be able to defend against common attacks. The left jab is a common attack used to strike and also to get the timing and distance to throw the right hand. One simple way to use the basics is to step back and a little to the right to allow the opponent's jab to miss and go over the left shoulder. This technique uses *Ichimonji no Kamae* as the defense. The left hand at the left shoulder is used to parry the punch if necessary away from the face. Notice that the forward left hand can counterpunch to the opponent's face.

NINJUTSU: ENDURING LEGACY

Parrying with a Cross Block

When an opponent throws a left jab at you, you can also parry it to the side by using *Jumonji no Kamae* and its inherent cross block. Step back and to the right slightly from *Ichimonji no Kamae* and turn your torso and the waist to the right catching the opponent's punching forearm with the left forearm of the cross block. Then immediately turn the torso to the left counterclockwise and strike into the opponent's neck with a left *Shuto* strike.

NINJUTSU: ENDURING LEGACY

Connecting Movements

I must emphasize the *kamae* are not static postures. One can flow from one *kamae* into another, but being in a specific *kamae* is not the end goal of movement. In fact, how one gets into *kamae* is what sets into motion movements that can be useful. As one moves the feet to step, power can be drawn from the legs and turn of the hips and shoulder to be used for further motion.

Cross Block, Shuto and Fudo Ken

The opponent tries to punch you with a right *Tsuki*. Step back and lightly to the right and block the punch with a left *Jodan Uke*. The opponent immediately throws a second punch with the left hand. Block the the punch by allowing the left arm to collapse and cross in front of you as you turn to the right. This is sometimes called a "*Jumonji Block*." As you block the hips and spine are loaded with kinetic energy. Suddenly, twist to the left and strike into the opponent's neck with a powerful left *Ura Shuto* strike to release this coiled energy. Follow this strike with a right *Fudo Ken* to the face.

NINJUTSU: ENDURING LEGACY

Keep Moving and Wrap Up the Opponent

Sometimes students get into trouble because they move to early and their opponents track their movments. Once a person commits to a punch or kick, they can't change the course of their attack. It is important to find the right timing. It is easier to judge one's timing against a single event, but it becomes much harder with sequential attacks.

In many techniques, the opponent is lured by his own aggression or confidence to advance into a trap. Sometimes the trap comes in the form of overcommitting to an attack and losing one's firm position. At times it may involve the attacker relying on the other person for balance or stability. There are other times when the aggressor may feel as though he has been tied up and there is no escape like a person ensnared in a rope or net.

Wrapping the Arm on a Second Punch

The opponent steps forward and punches with a right *Tsuki*. Step back and to the right and block with a left *Jodan Uke*. He steps forward and punches with a left *Tsuki*. Raise both arms up in *Hoko no Kamae* to block the punch. Wrap the opponent's left arm and throw him using *Musha Dori*.

NINJUTSU: ENDURING LEGACY

NINJUTSU: ENDURING LEGACY

Changing against Resistance

Resisting techniques using strength is probably not a wise thing to do. With speed and force ligaments and tendons can rupture or tear. Since this art accomplishes its work by using deception, the too obvious tendancy to force our will on our adversary is discouraged. Follow this way of thinking we tend to use more subtle means to achieve our ends.

The pictures on the following page shows *Tori* attempting to wrap up an *Uke's* left arm in *Musha Dori*. The *Uke* has straightened his arm and has evaded the technique. It is at this moment that many people would try and force the technique on using power. The *Tori* however sees that the *Uke's* arm being straight and pinned next to his body is vulnerable to hyperextension is struck loosely and suddenly without strength. *Tori* turns his hips and clips *Uke's* elbow from behind with his own arm. He then steps in front of *Uke's* left leg and sweeps it (*harai*) causing *Uke* to fall forward compounding the damage to his joints.

Conflicts rarely go according to plan. It is essential to be able to use effectively what the opponent offers you on a moment to moment basis.

NINJUTSU: ENDURING LEGACY

Making Techniques Seamless

After learning the basics one has to begin to apply them together in such a way that there are no breaks in one's movements. We all tend to go quickly with confidence through what is easy or familiar to us and slow down or stop when we hit areas of uncertainty. Conflict by its very nature is uncertain because your opponent will always have the ability to make his own decisions. A steady pace throughout each technique is important to develop a smooth flow and to take into account moment by moment what is required of you. As I have already stated, this art is about distance, angles and timing. It is not about techniques. Therefore, these "techniques" are done less like a recitation and more as an improvisation once one has learned the basics well.

Ura Gyaku to Omote Gyaku

The *Uke* will stand in a left *Ichimonji no Kamae* and punch at *Tori's* face with a right *Tsuki* as he stands in *Shizen no Kamae* (picture 1). As the punch comes in, *Tori* will step over slightly to the right and withdraw his left leg to the rear right as he brings his arm up in a right over left *Jumonji no Kamae*. *Tori's* left arm is inside the punch and his right hand and arm go over the top in a *Jumonji block* (picture 2). *Tori* will place his right thumb on the back of *Uke's* right hand and then turn his hips to the right as he uses his left arm to help turn Uke's arm over in an *Ura Gyaku*. *Tori* sinks down applying pressure with his left elbow and forearm to *Uke's* right arm (picture 3). *Uke* responds to having his form broken by trying to get low and standing up straight. *Tori* reaches over *Uke's* right arm and places his left thumb on the back of *Uke's* hand (picture 4). *Tori* will take an *Omote Gyaku* on the hand as he lifts it up and steps back to throw his opponent (picture 5). Once *Uke* is down *Tori* may apply an immobilization (picture 6).

NINJUTSU: ENDURING LEGACY

NINJUTSU: ENDURING LEGACY

Omote Gyaku to Ura Gyaku

Uke stands in a left *Ichimonji no Kamae* and steps forward with his right foot to punch with a right *Tsuki* at *Tori's* face. *Tori* stands in *Hira no Kamae* with arms open as if to invite *Uke* to attack (picture 1). Once the punch comes in *Tori* will step over slightly with his left foot and step back and to the left with his right foot as he intercepts the punching hand from the outside with his left hand (picture 2). *Tori* will place his thumb on the back of *Uke's* right hand and step across his body with his right foot. *Tori* suddenly turns and steps back with his left leg reversing directions to attempt to throw *Uke* with *Omote Gyaku*. *Uke* sees this coming and braces with a solid *kamae* (picture 3). *Tori* turns *Uke's* right hand and arms in a large clockwise circle using his left hand which turns the hold into an *Ura Gyaku* (picture 4). When *Uke's* hand reaches the 12:00 position, *Tori* will cross step left over right applying pain to the reversed hand (picture 5). *Tori* will press the knuckles of *Uke's* right hand towards the ground controlling *Uke* (picture 6).

NINJUTSU: ENDURING LEGACY

NINJUTSU: ENDURING LEGACY

戸隠流忍法体術
Togakure Ryu
Ninpo Taijutsu
The Hidden Door Lineage

Long ago a monk named *So-o* lived in a remote *Tendai* Buddhist monastery on *Mount Heizan*. One day he left and decided to live in a cave for three years for spiritual purification. This was not an uncommon practice for ascetics of Esoteric Buddhist followers. He is known for developing *Shugendo* (an Esoteric Buddhist sect) from his experiences. *Shugendo* is also called *Kaihogyo* and is similar to *Tendai* and *Shingon* sects of Buddhism.

A cluster of *Shugendo* followers originated in a village known as *Togakure* (*Togakushi*) in *Nagano* Prefecture. In 1165, a *samurai* named *Daisuke Nishina* was born. In the 1180's he fled a battle and went into *Iga*. There he met *Kain Doshi* who trained *Daisuke*. *Daisuke* combined the spiritual practices and martial arts practices which came primarily from *Gyokko Ryu* and *Koto Ryu* and formed *Togakure Ryu*.

Togakure Ryu is one of the nine lineages taught by *Grandmaster Masaaki Hatsumi*. Three of the nine lineages are not taught (at least not openly to any degree) by *Soke Hatsumi*. *Togakure Ryu* is one of the lineages that is specifically *Ninpo*. This means that although *ninja* of the past knew and practiced the other lineages of the *Bujinkan*, *Togakure Ryu* is a lineage not practiced by other styles outside of those schools who share a common history with either *Soke Takamatsu Toshisugu* or who were direct students of *Soke Hatsumi*.

Togakure Ryu Lineage Chart

Togakure (Nishina), Daisuke Oho circa 1161
Minamoto no Kanesada, Shima Kosanta 1180
Togakure, Goro 1200
Togakure, Kosanta
Koga, Kosanta
Kaneko, Tomoharu
Togakure, Ryuho
Togakure, Gakuun
Kido, Koseki
Iga, Tenryu
Ueno, Rihei
Ueno, Senri
Ueno, Manjiro
Iizuka, Saburo
Sawada, Goro
Ozaru, Ippei
Kimata, Hachiro
Kataoka, Heizaemon
Mori, Ugenta
Toda, Gobei
Kobe, Seiun
Momochi, Kobei
Tobari, Tenzen
Toda, Nobutsuna Seiryu Kwanyei circa 1624 - 1644
Toda, Nobuchika Fudo Manji circa 1658 - 1681
Toda, Kangoro Nobuyasu Tenna circa 1681 - 1704
Toda, Eisaburo Nobumasa Hoyei circa 1704 - 1711
Toda, Shinbei Masachika Shotoku circa 1711 - 1736
Toda, Shingoro Masayoshi Gembun circa 1736 - 1764
Toda, Daigoro Chikahide Meiwa circa 1764 - 1804
Toda, Daisaburo Chikashige Bunkwa circa 1804 - ?
Toda, Shinryuken Masamitsu ? - 1909 (b.1824 - d.1909)
Takamatsu, Toshitsugu 1907 - 1972 (b.1887 - d.1972)
Hatsumi, Masaaki 1958-Present (b. 1931)

構
Kamae (Postures)

In *Togakure Ryu* the *Kamae* are generally a little lower than in other *ryuha* within the *Bujinkan*. A *ninja* would want to avoid capture at all costs. Therefore, kamae are used which are lower to reduce visibility. Keep the feet wide, the center low, and the head back. The first kamae, *Ichi no Kamae* will seem similar to *Ichimonji no Kamae*. However notice how the body slightly leans back, and the rear hand conceals the face.

一之構
Ichi No Kamae (One Posture)

Ichi no Kamae is very similar to *Ichimonji no Kamae* in other *ryuha* of the *Bujinkan*. The major difference is that the feet are wider apart and the knees are flexed more deeply. The upper looks as though the person is leaning back to keep the head away from a potential attack. The left hand if forward points to the opponent's eyes, neck or heart. The front arm is slightly flexed. The rear arm guards the neck, hides a weapon or can be used to hide the face. The fingers of both hands are held straight but not rigid and are together. More weight is placed on the back leg than the front. The front leg should point in the direction of the opponent.

The leaning appearance the upper body combined with the wide positioning of the feet appears to some to be prohibitive of free movement. In *Togakure Ryu*, it is common to suddenly drop and roll away. If the feet are wide apart, one brings them together by getting down low and rolling away with *Ukemi*.

Ichi no Kamae

平一文字之構
Hira Ichimonji no Kamae (Flat Number One Posture)

This *kamae* is pretty much the same as *Hira no Kamae* as commonly practiced within the *Bujinkan*. One faces the opponent straight on with the legs spread slightly more than shoulder width and the arms out to the sides. One should bend the knees and lower the center a few inches. Arms should be out parallel to the ground. The toes point forward but slightly out to the sides. Keep the back straight and release tension from the shoulders.

Hira Ichimonji no Kamae

八文字之構
Hachimonji no Kamae (Number Eight Posture)

Stand with the feet the same way as *Ichi no Kamae*. The lead hand is also the same as *Ichi no Kamae*. The rear hand is held upwards above the head in a fist. The knuckles of that fist face the side of the head. The fist is held high and is not near the face. This *kamae* looks similar to what most would call *Doko no Kamae* in the *Bujinkan*. The rear arm is bent slightly. In this *kamae* one could hold *Metsubushi* up so as to throw it away from the body towards an attacker.

Hachimonji no Kamae

八方隠之構
Happo Gakure no Kamae (Eight Directions Hiding Posture)

This *kamae* too has feet positioned like *Ichi no Kamae*. This time both arms are held above the head and are ready to throw *Metsubushi*.

Happo Gakure no Kamae

遁之構
Tanso no Kamae (Hide and Run Away Posture)

Kneel as if in *Ichi no Kamae* with the right leg forward. Reach into the left side of the jacket at chest level with the right hand to pull out *Senban Shuriken* or *Metsubushi*. The left hand can grip the sword or be on guard.

Tosno no Kamae

体術受身型
Taijutsu Ukemi Gata
The Forms of Receiving an Attack

返し鳥
Kaeshi Dori (Bird Reversal)
Tori stands in *Ichi No Kamae*. *Uke* stands in *Dai Jodan No Kamae* (with his sword overhead). *Uke* steps forward with his right foot and cuts straight down. *Tori* moves forward and to the left dropping down low to a crouching position with his palms in front of and on both sides of *Uke's* forward right foot. *Tori* moves by stepping forward with the right foot and the left is down in a kneeling position. As the blade comes down it misses *Tori* and *Tori's* shoulder is around the level of *Uke's* right forearm. *Tori* can move *Uke's* forearm to the side by simply turning his hips. *Tori* will now jump up into *Uke*. He may use both feet to kick at the same time and then go back into a backward roll. *Tori* may also attack in a variety of other ways. *Tori* could kick and then punch or vice versa. The feeling of the technique is like the name suggests related to how a bird swoops down and then flies away suddenly. Therefore, when practicing this technique one should drop suddenly and then rise up suddenly making the attack with the feeling described here.

NINJUTSU: ENDURING LEGACY

Kaeshi Dori

NINJUTSU: ENDURING LEGACY

拳流し
Ken Nagare (Flowing Fist)

Tori stands in *Ichi No Kamae*. Uke stands in *Dai Jodan No Kamae*. *Uke* steps forward with his right foot and cuts straight down. *Tori* moves forward and to the left dropping down low to a crouching position with his palms in front of and on both sides of *Uke's* forward right foot. *Tori* moves by stepping forward with the right foot and the left is down in a kneeling position. *Tori* strikes *Uke* in *Suigetsu* (Solar Plexus) and then strikes *Uke's* right foot (*Toki*) with the *Shuko* (Hand Claws) of the left hand. As *Tori* begins to roll diagonally to the right and forward he uses the claws of the right hand on *Uke's* left foot. *Tori* rolls away with *Naname Zenpo Kaiten* (Diagonal Forward Roll.)

NINJUTSU: ENDURING LEGACY

Ken Nagare

NINJUTSU: ENDURING LEGACY

一之構
Ichi No Kamae (One Posture)

Tori stands in *Ichi No Kamae*. *Uke* stands in *Dai Jodan No Kamae*. *Uke* steps forward with his right foot and cuts straight down. *Tori* leaps forward and to the left diagonally and strikes *Uke* in the right temple with the edge of the *Shuko* (hand claws). He may then finish by using the claws of either hand.

This technique has variations as follows:

1. *Tori* leaps left and forward and uses his left hand to check *Uke's* right forearm while striking *Uke's* right temple with his right hand.
2. *Tori* leaps left and forward and uses his right hand to check *Uke's* right forearm while striking *Uke's* right temple with his left hand.
3. *Tori* leaps right and forward and uses his right hand to check *Uke's* left forearm while striking *Uke's* left temple with his left hand.
4. *Tori* leaps right and forward and uses his left hand to check *Uke's* left forearm while striking *Uke's* left temple with his right hand.

Ichi no Kamae

一刀捕り
Itto Dori (Seizing a Sword)

Tori stands in *Migi Ichi No Kamae*. *Uke* stands in *Dai Jodan No Kamae*. *Uke* steps forward with his right foot and cuts straight down. *Tori* steps forward with his left foot and raises his left hand catching the blade in the barbs of the *Shuko*. *Tori* then applies the other hand's *Shuko* to the claws in a solid grip and then twists the blade away to the side. *Tori* now strikes with a right *Ura Shuto* with the *Shuko* to *Uke's* face knocking him backwards. A variation of this is to apply a right kick to the groin at the moment the blade is turned to the side with both hands. Another variation is to take the blade away and turn it on *Uke*.

When practicing this technique or any other like it, do not use a live blade or real *Shuko*. In practice one must be aware that only the *Shuko* on the palm can be exposed to the sword. Many times people do not pull their fingers back sufficiently. Also, avoid catching the blade near the tip. Try to catch in in the middle because the speed of the blade faster at the end.

Itto Giri

NINJUTSU: ENDURING LEGACY

横蹴り
Yoko Geri (Side Kick)

Tori stands in *Hira Ichimonji No Kamae*. *Uke* stands in *Seigan No Kamae*. *Uke* steps forward with his right foot and thrusts in with a *Tsuki*. *Tori* shifts his weight to his left leg and leans to the left side. *Tori* lifts up his right foot and kicks under *Uke's* right elbow. Before *Tori's* foot comes down, he strikes low to *Suigetsu* (solar plexus) with a right *Fudo Ken*. The shifting of the weight in this technique to the left leg is to get off line of the thrust.

Yoko Geri

NINJUTSU: ENDURING LEGACY

一刀斬
Itto Giri (A Single Fatal Cut)

Uke stands in *Migi Seigan No Kamae* with his sword. *Uke* stands in *Dai Jodan No Kamae* with his sword. *Uke* steps forward with his right foot and cuts down with a straight cut to *Tori's* head. *Tori* steps back and to the left as he drops low. *Tori* swings his sword upwards across *Uke's Do* (Midsection) from a crouched position on his left knee. The goal is to get low under the opponent's cut and cut upwards with a low to high, left to right diagonal cut.

NINJUTSU: ENDURING LEGACY

Itto Giri

NINJUTSU: ENDURING LEGACY

忍返型
Shinobi Gaeshi Gata
Forms of Stealth

重返
Shige Gaeshi (Serious Turn)

This technique is for hiding and getting over a wall that is high. One begins by running up the wall and grabbing the top with both hands. Then, pull your body up and swing one leg over to get a foot on top of the wall. Use this hold to pull your body up so that you lay flat on top of the wall. The body should be horizontal on top of the wall. Keep the arms and legs together straight and lay in place motionless so as not to be detected.

This technique teaches us that at times it is better to remain still. What is not looked for often is not seen.

重捕
Shige Tori (Serious Capture)

From the *Kasane Gaesh*i position on top of the wall, swing the legs down and kick someone walking by. Then, swing the pelvis over to the other side of the wall and jump down to escape. In this technique, the arms hold on to the wall and the pelvis swings from one side of the wall to the other. This technique teaches us how react when we have been discovered. By that I mean, strike hard and disappear again while the enemy is recovering.

猿飛
Saru Tobi (Limb Flying)

While being pursued the *ninja* would find a branch of a tree high enough to jump up and catch. The *ninja* would catch the branch with both hands and pull himself up. He would then use this branch to get to a higher branch to hide in within the tree. From this lookout he could hide, gather intelligence, or use weapons. A deeper interpretation of this technique is to go beyond the obvious hiding place. The first branch is like a stepping-stone to the next level. This technique teaches us to retreat to the high ground and wait for the best time to take advantage of our position.

横流し
Yoko Nagashi (Side Flow)

When confronted by two attackers the goal is to position them by using steps. As the *ninja* adjusted his steps so would the attackers. In this technique, the *ninja* has an attacker in front of him and one behind him a few feet away. The *ninja* is in the middle or has moved to get himself and the attackers in this position. The *ninja* will throw *metsubushi* or other distraction at the attacker behind him knowing the attacker in front will find this as an opening and begin his attack. When the attacker in front comes in the *ninja* does *Yoko Nagare* (Side Flow Roll) out of the line of attack. The goal is to get the attacker in front to accidentally cut or stab the attacker from behind. The attacker in front must fully commit to his attack and the right distance to the two attackers will interfere with one another. Getting the attackers to mistakenly attack each other is the essence of this technique. After rolling away, the ninja can throw *Senban Shuriken* or use other weapons but must maintain *Zanshin*.

From this technique we learn how to turn our enemies against one another.

後ろ流し
Ushiro Nagashi (Backwards Flow)

When the *ninja* is confronted with attackers at close range he may roll backwards and throw *metsubushi* or *shuriken* from a kneeling position. Jumps and flips would startle attackers long enough for the *ninja* to escape or to mount a surprise attack. This technique teaches us that retreat can be used as an offensive plan of action.

秘伝型
Hiden Gata
Secret Forms

中返し
Naka Gaeshi (Center Flow)

When being pursued, the ninja startles the attackers by doing consecutive *Kuten* (handsprings) and then runs away.

横返し
Yoko Gaeshi (Side Flow)

When being pursued, the *ninja* startles the attackers by doing consecutive *Oten* (Cartwheels) and then runs away. One may also carry weapons in the hands or pick up weapons from the ground while doing *Oten*. Long weapons like a staff or spear may be used to assist in doing the Oten or used to thrust as one flips over. *Naka Gaeshi* and *Yoko Gaeshi* both teach us to be free enough to do the unexpected. In life, unpredictable actions make our strategies obscure to our adversaries. This similar to the roll done to the side shown earlier in this book.

飛違
Tobi Chigai (Flying By)

Tobi Chigai involves methods for climbing trees using *Shuko* (Hand Claws). They could be used on the hands of feet to get up into trees to hide, set up an ambush or collect information. *Shoten no Jutsu* is the art of climbing up flat surfaces. *Shoten no Jutsu* is generally practiced by running up inclines with progressively steeper surfaces. To get higher up the tree, the *ninja* would make a running jump and then grip the bark with the *Shuko*. This technique teaches us to sum up a situation from a remote perspective for the purpose of a broader view.

銛盤投げ
Senban Nage (Throwing Flat Shuriken)

Senban Shuriken are four pointed, flat throwing discs made of steel. They are generally carried in the jacket. Traditionally, nine was the number carried, but this may be more myth than truth. They were removed with the left hand and held in the right palm at the waist. To practice this technique, assume *Tanso no Kamae* and throw the *shuriken* with a flick of the wrist. If one can flick the *shuriken* so that they spin in place then they can be propelled later with a rocking motion which involves the whole arm. *Shuriken* were used as a painful but probably not fetal deterrent for anyone pursuing a fleeing *ninja*. This technique teaches how to thwart the enemy to give up chase. In life repeated set backs in the pursuit of a goal causes people who lack resolve to give up.

一刀斬
Itto Giri (A Single Fatal Cut)

An injured *ninja* who is unable to walk or get away as a last resort would throw his sword. This technique involves methods of throwing the sword while sitting or lying down in various positions and distances. Knives, daggers or other concealed blades would be used for the same purpose. Capture for a *ninja* would mean certain death. This technique employs the spirit of fighting until the bitter end without accepting defeat.

返し
Kiri Gaeshi (Cutting Reversal)

When confronted with a single swordsman, the *ninja* could assume *Naka Seigan* (similar to *Chudan no Kamae*) with his sword pointed level and directly pointed ahead. As his opponent gets into *Seigan no Kamae* sword held at arms length with the tip pointed at the eyes, the *ninja* would parry the sword to the side an step forward and diagonally to cut across the opponent's midsection. The sword in this technique acts as a probe and then cuts in. As a strategy, this technique teaches us to bide our time, look for weaknesses in our enemy's defenses and move forward boldly to end the conflict.

捨身
Sutemi (To Sacrifice One's Life)

When surrounded, the *ninja* looked for the leader. The leader could be cut down first and or the weakest person near the leader. The ninja would clear an opening in this way and escape. The idea of this technique is to find the weakest link in the chain and escape through the opening to reconfigure the arrangement of attackers so that one is not surrounded. This technique teaches us to examine the strengths and weakness of our adversary's strategies and breakthrough to necessitate regrouping or the development of a different strategy even it at great personal risk.

竄逃遁甲之型
Santo Tonko No Gata
(Hiding, Running Away, and Escaping Patterns)

This section deals with moments in which *a ninja* has been grabbed by an attacker and must quickly flee. The use of *Senban Shuko*, and *Metsubushi* are found among these techniques. When grabbed the *ninja* responds by using the *Shuko*. This generally means attacking the hand that has grabbed among other places. These techniques end with the *ninja* throwing the opponent, bursting *Metsubushi* into his eyes, and then running for cover. While practicing use rubber or leather *Shuko* and if you like, fill plastic eggs with confetti or flour for safety purposes.

The manner in which the techniques begin is quite curious. The opponent grabs the wrist or forearm and pulls as if to try and take the other person somewhere. In these techniques, the feet form an "L-shaped" configuration in which the front foot is forward and the rear foot points out to the side. The hand being pulled is extended forward and kept relaxed. For practicing the techniques in the traditional manner, both the *Uke* and *Tori* will open and raise their rear hands almost in the manner of *Hoko* or *Doko no Kamae*. As one is pulled a total of three steps are taken by the *Uke*. The technique happens as *Uke* pulls back on the third step. *Tori* mirrors *Uke's* steps to the rear by stepping forward. Be careful not to bob up and down too much as you step. At first this seems awkward and contrived, but it is actually teaching how to mirror your opponent's movements in motion and to develop the timing necessary to do technique without a pause. Ideally, one should develop the feeling of floating as one is pulled, and as a result these techniques when done properly become very dynamic.

片腕遁走之型
Kata Ude Tonso No Kata (Single Wrist Escape Pattern)

The opponent grabs *Tori's* right forearm with his right hand and pulls as he steps back three steps. On the *Uke's* third step *Tori* seizes the opponent's right forearm and sinks the barbs of the *Shuko* into his flesh. At the same time he kicks up into the groin with the right forward foot. Combined, these two activities raise the opponent's heels and right elbow up bending him forward and making him unstable. *Tori* then goes under the *Uke's* right arm, pivots and turns around. *Tori* places barbs of the left *Shuko* into the tricep of *Uke's* right arm. *Tori* goes down to his left knee and projects *Uke* forward into a roll or fall face first. *Tori* immobilizes the opponent, applies *Metsubushi* or escapes.

Kata Ude Tonso no Kata

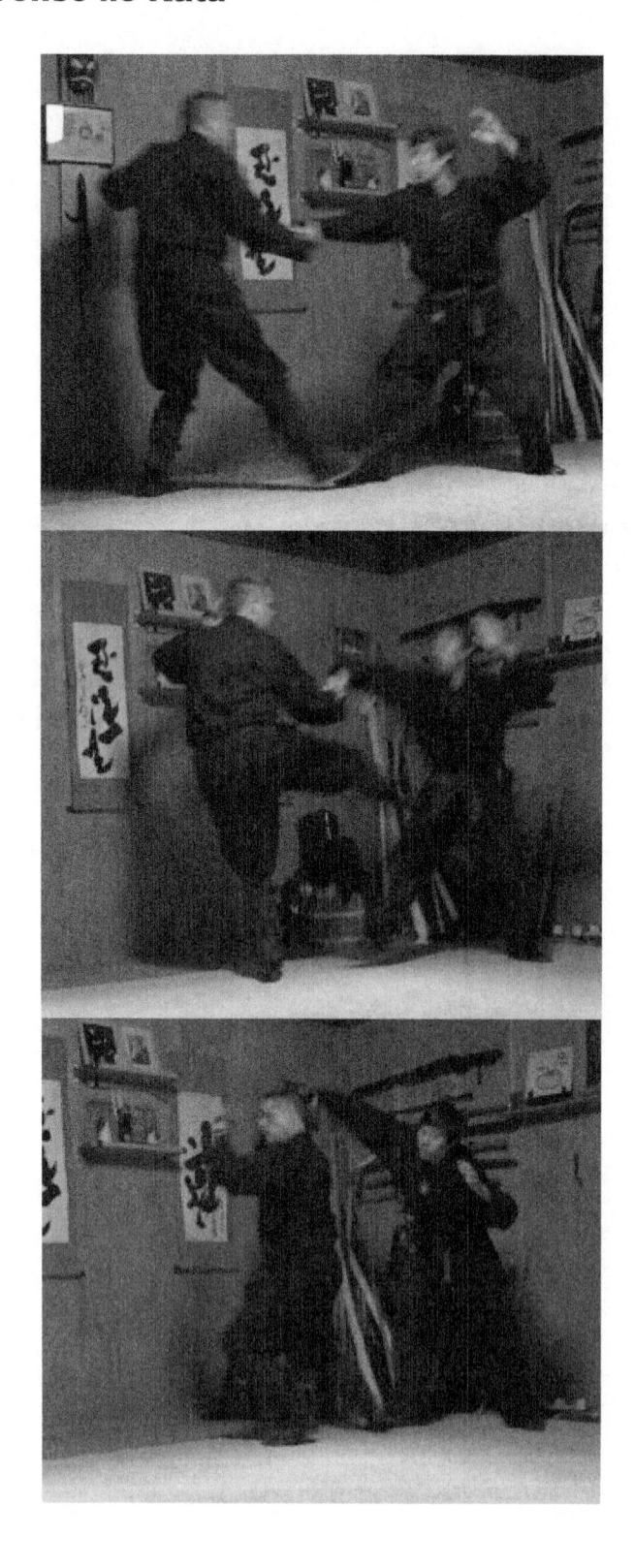

NINJUTSU: ENDURING LEGACY

左遁走之型
Hidari Tonso No Kata (Left Escape Pattern)

The opponent grabs *Tori's* left wrist with his right hand and pulls as he steps back three steps. On the *Uke's* third step *Tori* seizes the opponent's right forearm from below as described previously with the *Shuko*. *Tori* then kicks up into *Uke's* groin with the right foot, and seizes *Uke's* clothing at the right shoulder with his right hand. As *Uke* is light on his feet from the kick, *Tori* steps back with right foot before putting the kicking leg down. *Tori's* will put his right knee down as he raises *Uke's* right hand up and pulls forward and down on *Uke's* shoulder. *Uke* goes face first to the ground. *Tori* immobilizes the opponent, applies *Metsubushi* or escapes.

Hidari Tonso No Kata

NINJUTSU: ENDURING LEGACY

左腕遁走之型
Hidari Ude Tonso No Kata (Left Wrist Escape Pattern)

The opponent grabs *Tori's* left forearm with his left hand and pulls as he steps back three steps. On the *Uke's* third step *Tori* seizes the opponent's left forearm and sinks the barbs of the *Shuko* into his flesh. *Tori* raises *Uke's* left forearm up so that the elbow is pointing up and then kicks into *Uke's* groin with the left foot. As *Uke* is light on his feet *Tori* steps to the outside of *Uke's* left foot and throws *Uke* down on his back as *Tori* sinks to his right knee. *Tori* immobilizes the opponent, applies *Metsubushi* or escapes.

Hidari Ude Tonso No Kata

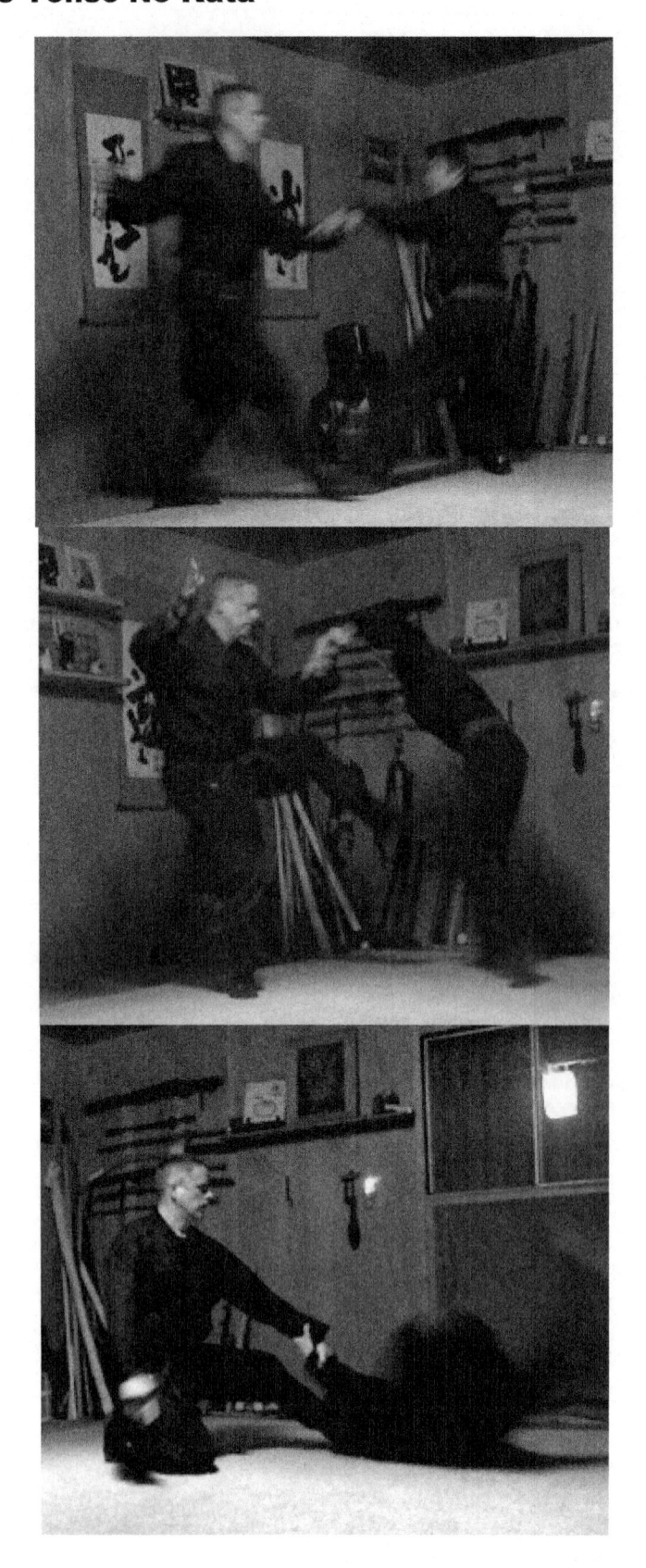

右遁走之型
Migi Tonso No Kata (Right Escape Pattern)

The opponent grabs *Tori's* right wrist with his left hand and pulls as he steps back three steps. On the *Uke's* third step *Tori* circles his right hand counterclockwise around *Uke's* left hand and attempts to place his right palm on the back of *Uke's* left, bent elbow. *Tori* will apply a *Muso Dori* type of hold on *Uke's* left elbow as he kicks *Uke* with his left foot in the thigh or solar plexus. Before putting the left kicking foot down, *Tori* will step back with the left leg going down to his left knee causing *Uke* to fall forward face first. *Tori* immobilizes the opponent, applies *Metsubushi* or escapes.

Migi Tonso No Kata

NINJUTSU: ENDURING LEGACY

右手首筋遁走之型
Migi Tekubi Suji Tonso No Kata (Right Forearm Escape Pattern)

Tori is walking along and *Uke* uses his right hand to grab *Tori* by the collar from behind. Once *Uke* has grabbed *Tori*, he pulls back. As *Uke* pulls back *Tori* follows the motion back striking *Uke* in *Suigetsu* (Solar Plexus) with a left elbow strike. At the same time *Tori* seizes the grabbing hand with his own right hand behind his back. *Tori* grabs *Uke's* hand in an *Ura Gyaku* type of grab. *Tori* will then go under *Uke's* right arm and step back with his left foot. This throws *Uke* forward with an *Ura Gyaku Dori* applied to his wrist. Once *Uke* is down, *Tori* takes out a *Metsubushi* egg, cracks it open and throws it into *Uke's* eyes before running away for cover.

左手首筋遁走之型
Hidari Tekubi Suji Tonso No Kata (Left Forearm Escape Pattern)

This is exactly the same as the previous technique except it is done on the opposite side.

This next group of techniques require that *Tori* wear *Shuko* (hand claws) and face Uke who is wielding a sword. All of these techniques end with throwing *Metsubushi*.

NINJUTSU: ENDURING LEGACY

NINJUTSU: ENDURING LEGACY

当込遁走之型
Ate Komi Tonso No Kata (Count On Escape Patterns)

Tori stands in *Hidari Hachimonji No Kamae*. *Uke* stands in *Dai Jodan No Kamae*. As *Uke* steps forward with his right foot and cuts straight down, *Tori* will step forward with his right foot and punch low from a kneeling position on his left knee to *Suigetsu*. By sinking low and moving off line to the left, *Tori* avoids the cut. *Tori* will then stand up and throw *Metsubushi* before running away.

小手打遁走之型
Kote Uchi Tonso No Kata (Striking the Wrist Escape Pattern)

Tori stands in *Hidari Hachimonji No Kamae*. *Uke* stands in *Dai Jodan No Kamae*. As *Uke* steps forward with the right foot and cuts straight down, *Tori* leaps diagonally to the left and forward off line and at the same time strikes down on *Nagare*. *Nagare* is the *kyusho* nerve point found around the meaty part of the brachioradialis muscle. *Tori* hits this point with the outer edge of the *Shuko* like an *Ura Shuto*. This causes *Uke* to drop his sword. *Tori* crouches in place and strikes with his right palm to *Uke's Suigetsu* or ribs. As *Uke* falls backwards to the ground, *Tori* throws *Metsubushi* into *Uke's* eyes and runs away.

左打遁走之型
Migi Uchi Tonso No Kata (Striking from the Right Escape Pattern)

Tori stands in *Hidari Hachimonji No Kamae*. *Uke* stands in *Seigan No Kamae*. *Uke* thrusts by sliding his lead foot forward. *Tori* leaps diagonally forward and to the left to get off line while at the same time striking *Uke's* left *Nagare* with a downward *Ura Shuto*. *Tori* grabs the *Tsuka* (Sword Hilt) with his left hand and take the blade away. *Tori* steps back and turn the blade over before throwing *Metsubushi* into *Uke's* eyes and running away. The blade is turned over to face *Uke* in case he tries to get it back or if *Tori* needs to use it on *Uke*.

The next group of techniques involves a *ninja* faced with multiple attackers. The *ninja's* goal is to manage the positions of each attacker relative to each other so that *Metsubushi* can be thrown effectively and an escape can be made.

左右雲隠之型
Sayu Kumo Gakure No Kata (Left and Right Escaping in a Cloud Pattern)

The *ninja* has found himself confronted with two swordsman in front of him. At first they are apart. The *ninja* moves so that the swordsmen will get closer to each other. When they are a few feet apart, the *ninja* will throw *Metsubushi* using *Happo Gakure no Kamae* at both swordsman and strike each before rolling away and fleeing. If the swordsmen are too far apart, *Shuriken* may be thrown if available.

攻勢雲隠之型
Kosei Kiri Gakure No Kata (Attacking the Leader Cloud Hiding Pattern)

The *ninja* faces a few swordsmen in front of him. His goal is to break through and flee. To do this he must create a diversion and make a hole in their formation. To begin the *ninja* will take out a stack of *Senban Shuriken* and hold them in his right hand and start throwing them at each of the swordsmen to keep them at bay from *Tanso No Kamae* or while standing. Some of the swordsmen may flinch or move creating an opening. The *ninja* escapes through the opening by throwing *Metsubushi* at the two swordsmen standing closest to him as he attempts to pass their perimeter.

八方霧隠之型
Happo Kuri Gakure No Kata (Fog In All Directions Hiding Pattern)

The *ninja* finds himself facing three swordsmen from the front and two more pulling up from the rear. The *ninja* cannot easily pass in either direction. The *ninja* throws *Senban Shuriken* at the three in front and while they are flinching, he quickly turns and throws *Metsubushi* at the other two. The *ninja* then flees by running away either to the left or to the right.

五遁之術

Goton no Jutsu
Five Escape Arts

In the philosophies of East Asia, the Five Elements play an essential role in understanding the workings of nature. These concepts originated in China and may have come to Japan in the late *T'ang* Dynasty along with Buddhism. Buddhism and Taoism in certain respects co-mingled in China with regard to certain aspects of cosmology. The Five Elements is such an example. To understand what is meant by the Five Elements we need to get a more basic understanding of some other key concepts first.

A Linear View of Time

Every day life could be looked at as following a path. That path may have its ups and downs but overall there is a balance which keeps life moving on. These differences make life like a line with curves going up and down. In this way, we can think of a life as a wave pattern similar to what we think of in terms of electricity. It is believed that more ups and downs create a disruptive pattern and life is shortened. This is a Taoist notion of how to have harmony in life, follow the natural course or life and to extend life as far as possible.

A Cyclical View of Life

If we were to walk across a continent we would probably never notice the curvature of the planet. Such observations are made at a distance. If we distance ourselves from our own lives we may notice that they are cyclical in a generational sense although they may appear linear from birth to death in an individual sense. Patterns of growth, maturity, decline, and renewal can be seen in all facets of nature.

Complimenting Opposites

The highs and lows of life mentioned earlier compliment one another. Opposites seem to attract and this acts as a generating force of differentiation in life and in nature. In and Yo, sometimes called *Yin* and *Yang* in Chinese, represent this principle. For instance, we can appreciate the value of "day" because we know "night." Male and female, high and low, positive and negative etc....are all examples of how nature can be seen as having polarities that necessitates a need for balance somewhere in between the extremes. Therefore, it is understood in Taoist cosmology that every system contains polar opposites which act as balancing forces for the whole system.

Five Elemental Phases of Cycles

The five elements in this case are Earth, Water, Metal, Fire, and Wood. This should not be confused with the elements of Earth, Water, Fire, Wind and Void as in the *San Shin No Kata*. Water, Metal, Fire and Wood naturally occur on Earth. Earth is referred to as a centering force which acts upon the other four elements. If one of the four elements is dominant then Earth as a force yields. When any of the four elements are becoming weak, the Earth force causes a new phase in which transition, growth or change occurs. This in turn affects all of the other elements. Like the children's game of "Rock, Paper, Scissors," no one element dominates all of the others. One element may exert more influence on another but this influence at times wanes. The study of these elements is a profound study of the workings of nature. It is very broad in scope and its influence has affected everything from Traditional Chinese Medicine to military strategy.

Ninja clans were noted for their ability to play upon the common superstitions of others at the time. A *ninja's* understanding of the Five Elements was practical and not dogmatic or superstitious. In other words, a *ninja* would have applied "the principles" of the five elements, but would not have become superstitious by using them. For instance, a day to attack a castle would be picked based on practical factors primarily like the weather, time, terrain etc... rather than celestial signs or other perceived omens.

Living in today's modern world with its modern conveniences has in effect removed us from nature to a degree in which the understanding and necessity of using the *Godai* (Five Elements) in its historical sense. With that said, the essence of the techniques is passed down to us embodying principles that are timeless. If we want to be able to apply these elements, we might first start by understanding the properties of each element and what we know about them if we wish to incorporate them into strategy.

Water can be……..
Warm and inviting
So hot that it is avoided
So cold that is is avoided
Frozen
Boiling
A mist
Clouded and murky
Flowing
Drops or as big as oceans
Stagnant
Colored
A home for living creatures
A hiding place
A thirst quencher
Many more things

Do you see how each of these could be applied to a strategy?
If you can think of Earth, Fire, Metal and Wood in the same way, the possibilities become endless.

水遁之術
Sui Ton No Jutsu
Water Escape Arts

Sui Ton No Jutsu is the art of using water for evasion, escape, concealment and attacking. Water takes on the forms of solids, liquids and gases. These natural states of matter could also be used to one's advantage.

立ち泳ぎ
Tachi Oyogi
(Swimming While Standing)

This is a method of swimming which involves treading water in a standing position. This would be done by bending a knee, lifting up the leg, and turning the foot and leg in circles under the water. The body bobs up and down and the circular motion helps the *ninja* to tread water and keep his head afloat. The hands are free but may be used to move about if necessary. The *sageo* (cord attached to sword case) could be tied around the neck so a sword would not be lost in a current or daggers could be carried in the mouth like a pirate. This method is not meant to cover distance, but rather to stay in place in still water or a light current.

抜き手
Nuki Te (Swimming with Hands Free)

The legs kick out like a frog leaping. The arms make a crawling motion. Propulsion comes from the thrust of the feet. This causes a glide. The *ninja* would then paddle with the arms. The flexion and extension of the body during propulsion and glide phases must be timed with the breathing. A short sword or dagger might also be carried in the mouth using this stroke.

あおり平
Aori Hira (Flat Scissor Stroke)

This method of swimming is similar to the sidestroke. The legs make a frog-like propulsion followed by scissoring and paddling of the feet. The body seems to lean forward as one goes through the water sideways, and the lead hand points through the water during the glide phases.

捕縛泳ぎ
Ho Baku Oyogi (Swimming Tied Up)

This method of swimming was used if one had been arrested and tied up by the hands or feet. To survive, one would need to tread water by undulating in a wave-like motion like a fish. It is perhaps easier to do this face up keeping the head above water.

毒水鉄砲
Doku Mizu Teppo (Toxic Water Gun)

A plunger was pushed through a completely hollow bamboo tube filled with water. The result was water forced out of the tube under pressure. Of course this is very primitive. If the plunger does not fit snuggly in the tube, pressure is lost and the propulsion of water is weaker. If the tube is filled with toxic water, there is the risk of leaking. With the invention of modern plastics, a Super Soaker® squirt gun would work much better. It too however is not entirely free of malfunction with substances as risky as toxins.

欺弈搔乱
Hen Kaku Ran
(Deceiving by Stirring Up Confusion)

If a *ninja* were being pursued near the banks of a river or stream, he could throw a large rock into the water that would make a splash sounding like a human taking a dive. The pursuers would think that the runaway had jumped in and start looking in the water. The *ninja* would then run the other way.

水蜘蛛
Mizu Gumo (Water Spider)

The *Mizu Gumo* was a floatation device consisting of five inflatable sections. Four sections were sewn in such a way that when roped together would form a large doughnut shape that would fit around the body like an innertube. One would sit on the fifth section in the middle. Hundreds of years ago rubber tires had not been invented which would allow one to put an inner tube around the waist and move about in the water. This was the equivalent of that. Hides of some sort were more than likely used, and the inflated sections could be deflated and packed easily for land travel. A paddle was sometimes carried consisting of a bamboo shaft a few feet long with a concealed bamboo folding fan in one end that made the end of the paddle. The fan was attached to a rope or cord that could be used to rope things or swung as a weapon.

水中器
Sui Chuki (Underwater Utensil)

The *Sui Chuki* was a hollow bamboo tube used to breathe under water. It could vary in length and width depending on whether of not it was carried a head of time or found and used when needed. Used in open areas of water it would likely be seen, and so hidden under things like plants, and rocks around shorelines, it would be harder to spot. One would hold the tube in the mouth with one hand and pinch the nose with the other as one looked up through the surface of the water with the tube in the mouth. This is basically a primitive snorkeling apparatus. With the invention of flexible rubber tubing and moldable plastics, we now have far superior equipment than what the *ninja* would have been using.

金遁之術

Kin Ton No Jutsu
Metal Escape Arts

Kin Ton No Jutsu encompasses the use of sound and light for the purpose of hiding, infiltration, concealment and attack. There is an emphasis on the use of metal objects to accomplish this and deceiving the opponent's senses.

谺之法

Kodama no Ho (Use of Tree Spirits)

Kodama no Ho uses loud noises to startle an opponent. This is sometimes done by hitting two objects together or dropping an object. Noises could also be used as signals. The name *Kodama* for this principle is a rare word in Japanese. It has two meanings. One meaning is an echo and the other is a tree spirit. Perhaps this rare word could bring to mind a simple Japanese peasant's fear of phantoms deep in the forest. Assuming he was alone, such a peasant, or *samurai* for that matter, would be quite alarmed if he heard the cry of a tengu.

Things that go bump in the night send chills down our spine.

Some sounds naturally cause fear in humans because we know the dangers they potentially bring. Here are some examples of sounds are early ancestors passed on to us:

1. The roar of an animal like a lion or tiger near us
2. The sound of thunder nearby
3. The crashing of a felled tree in close proximity
4. The sounds of ghosts
5. The crackling noises of an inferno
6. Cries for help
7. Screams

As times changed the dangers of technology has given rise to noises that inspire fear or anxiety such as:

1. The roar of cannons or blasts of gunfire
2. The sound of sirens
3. The sound of alarms
4. Cars backfiring
5. Low flying planes going by

In our modern world, there are some sound diversions consistent with the spirit of *Togakure Ryu*. These examples should be studied as examples of how not to be taken by surprise by the enemy.

I remember when Manuel Noriega was captured by American forces in Panama during the 80's. He was held up in a building and American forces blasted rock music at the building to make his existence miserable. He eventually gave up. The military used the noise as a type of psychological warfare to gain Noriega's capture. This is just one way to creatively use this element.

光之法（合図）
Hikari no Ho -Aizu
(Use of Light for Signaling)

Mirrors can be used to catch reflections of sunlight and create signals by code. The mirror can be moved in a particular way or the hand can pass in front of the mirror creating a flickering light. Swords have reflective surfaces that could be used the same way.

光之法（目潰し）
Hikari no Ho-Metsubushi
(Use of Light for Blinding)

Mirrors or reflections from swords can also be used for blinding an opponent long enough to get away, or to win in combat. The distraction creates a divergence of the senses in which the ninja can exploit.

陰陽之法
In Yo No Ho
(Use of Shadow and Light)

The human eye contains a pupil which regulates how much light can enter the eye. When a person is in bright light his or her eyes cannot adjust instantaneously to complete darkness. The same is true for someone who is in darkness and then is exposed suddenly to bright light. The mind can become confused or dazed at such times as the eyes catch up and relate information to the brain. By turning on or off a light at the right time, an opponent could be blinding momentarily long enough to get away.

木遁之術
Moku Ton No Jutsu
Wood Escape Arts

Moku Ton No Jutsu involves the use of plants, bushes, trees and wood for the purposes of hiding, escape, attack, infiltration and creating confusion. Forms are lost as their edges break up behind the cover of many leaves.

偽装之法
Gi So No Ho (Camouflage Method)

Gi So No Ho encompasses methods for hiding in wait using camouflage made of plants. The human form is easily recognizable and therefore to hide, it is best to break up the body's outline to the observer's eye. This was done by *ninja* by tying string around their torso and legs and then inserting pieces of plants from the area under the string. The plant sections could be one foot to three feet long and put all over the body. It was important to use fresh plants and plants that naturally grow in the area. When one hid, it would be natural to go to areas where the same type of plants could be found. The plants had the ability to not only color the person like the surrounding environment, but also to break up the lines of the human form so that the *ninja* could naturally blend in.

鶉（うずら）隠之法
Uzura Gakure No Ho
(Hiding Like a Quail Method)

Quails hide under cover and then suddenly fly away. This is the feeling of *Uzura Gakure no Ho*. This technique places the *ninja* in plant cover hidden among trees, vines or shrubs and then when the enemy approaches nearby, the *ninja* comes out suddenly and cuts down the enemy.

目潰（めつぶし）之法
Metsubushi No Ho (Blinding Method)

Before being confronted with a swordsman, the *ninja* would find a small leafy branch to pull behind him while holding the sword with the other hand. When the swordsman attacked the branch would be whipped into the swordsman's face surprising him and providing an opening to cut him down with the *ninja*'s sword.

偽変木遁之法
Ho Hen Moku Ton No Ho
(Changing to Something Fake Method)

When a *ninja* was pursued on foot he used a tactic in which he would stop and vigorously shake the branches of a tree. The pursuer would hear this, and then look carefully up in the trees for the *ninja*. At this time, the *ninja* would quietly come out of hiding and cut the person down.

倒木偽変之法
To Boku Gi Hen No Ho
(Knocking Down Wood Camouflage Method)

Ninjas would sometimes stack cut bamboo poles next to a tree along a road or other pathway where the enemy would travel. The *ninja* would hide in the same tree or tie a thin rope to the tops of the poles from a nearby tree. When the enemy came down the road the *ninja* would knock over the bamboo poles on the enemy creating injury and chaos. The *ninja* would then jump down and cut down his enemies in the confusion.

土遁之術
Do Ton No Jutsu
Earth Escape Arts

Do Ton No Jutsu involves the use of the ground for hiding, infiltration, escape, attack and creating confusion. These methods can included digging into the ground to hide, the use of terrain and other elements of the landscape.

目潰（めつぶし）之法
Metsubushi No Ho

When confronted with an attacker such as a swordsman, the *ninja* would often kick or throw sand or dirt in the attacker's face. The *ninja* would dig his toes under loose dirt and kick it up in the attacker's face. Some techniques in *Togakure Ryu* are entries for attacks in which the *ninja* ducks down low close to the ground before spring up to cut down the opponent. It is at such times that dirt or sand is picked up. The *ninja* would not be limited to sand or dirt. Pepper from a table could be used these days with great effect. Rocks, gravel and pebbles also work nicely.

土竜（もぐり）之法
Moguri no Ho (Earthworm Method)

This technique involves hiding in a hole in the ground. The *ninja* may find a natural spot partially or completely covered on the sides and lay plants or other debris over his body as he hides in waiting for the enemy. Once the enemy passes by, the *ninja* would cut the person as they passed by.

Although this method seems labor intensive and impractical in this day and age, I can think of two examples in which this methodology has been applied in modern combat. The first is the inventive weapons of the *Viet Cong* during the Viet Nam War. At least 10% of all American casualties in Viet Nam were believed to be caused by booby traps. One of the most common was punji sticks. A hole was dug into ground a few feet deep. Sharpened sticks or sharpened metal rods were placed into the ground at the bottom of the pit. The pit was then covered up with palm branches, grass and other things. As a person stepped on to the covering, the person fell in and was impaled on the sticks. To add insult to injury.dung was placed on the ends of the sticks to poison the blood. Another example of *Moguri no Ho* used by *Viet Cong* involves a type of primitive land mine. A narrow bamboo tube was attached vertically over a bullet standing straight up. Below the bullet was a nail driven through a board that provided the base for the whole mechanism. The whole thing was buried just below the surface of the ground and covered up. When a soldier stepped on the bamboo it pressed the bullet into the nail and exploded. This would shoot the soldier in the foot. Such tactics seem old fashioned to most people in America who are used to warfare fought with maximum use of technology. However, without technology, guerilla fighters around the world take advantage of simple methods like this to defeat their enemies.

The second example of *Mogori no Ho* that comes to mind is how during the Gulf War Iraqi soldiers in tanks would dig into the sand with their tanks to be blanketed by the desert floor. They would wait ready for ambush. Unfortunately, this tactic did not work because of American equipment capable of reading changes in heat in an area. The heat emittting from the Iraqi tanks was enough to alert American forces to their location, and mark them for destruction. This too is an example of using the five elements. Primarily this example is using *Ka Ton No Jutsu* which is the "Art of Using Fire." Because heat was sensed, it fits into this category.

落花之法
Haku No Ho (Falling Leaves Method)

If an enemy came into the *ninja*'s encampment, a hole might be dug out to keep prisoners in or just to trap them and then cut them down right away. The *ninja* would run or move in a direction that would lure the enemy into a hole in the ground that was covered over so the enemy would fall down inside and be trapped.

As mentioned earlier, the *Viet Cong* used methods burying traps. They also used *Haku No Ho*. When retreating, the *Viet Cong* would lead American soldiers into areas with booby traps or hand made mines. These types of ordinance were usually left behind by Americans and used trip wires to be activated. The goal of course for the Viet Cong was the same as the *ninja*'s goal. Since the traps are not everywhere, one must lead the enemy to the trap.

隱遁之法
Gakure Ton No Ho (Hiding Method)

After a *ninja* had cut down an enemy he realized that he must flee the area quickly as there might be others who will also begin the pursuit. The *ninja* would look for places that provided covering. Spaces between rocks, ditches, caves, and tunnels provided temporary shelter while hiding.

During the *Viet Nam War* it seemed at times the *Viet Cong* would suddenly appear and then disappear. Because of extensive tunneling throughout the country, it made it possible for these soldiers to fight and then hide or relocate quickly. Routine bombing raids which seemed to fit the schedule of the pilots provided predictable times to be in an out of the tunnels. Although enormous amount of ordinance were dropped on the *Viet Cong*, they remained resilient and this is one of the reasons.

I think the lesson to be learned from this technique is that if you might have to run, know where you will run and be prepared beforehand.

火遁之術
Ka Ton No Jutsu
Fire Escape Arts

Ka Ton No Jutsu uses fire, heat and boiling substances for attack, escape, deception and infiltration. *Ninjas* were masters at starting fires to create chaos so that fortifications could be attacked. The methods listed here are a sampling of the ingenuity used by *ninja*.

火攻（ぜい）之法
Hi Zeme No Ho (Fire Gauntlet Method)

Once an enemy has been lead into an area in which a perimeter can be established, the surrounding area is set on fire and the enemy is left to burn. If the enemy tries to escape the perimeter each soldier is cut down as he escapes. In this technique, we learn that fire cannot annihilate completely, and can also be used to bring the enemy out into the open. In a broader sense, in life we can set up a situation which exposes our enemy's intentions and brings them to surface to be examined.

熱湯攻（ぜい）之法
Netto Zeme No Ho
(Boiling Water Gauntlet Method)

If an enemy approached the *ninja's* encampment by surprise, the *ninja* could throw boiling water from the fire onto the enemy's face. The *ninja* could then cut down the enemy or run away. Water was often kept boiling for making tea so this made a very accessible ally and tool. Throughout history boiling water or oil has been used to pour on people during seiges on castles and could also be done by one person at a campfire using the same principle. This technique could easily be incorporated into modern times. For instance, if one is being robbed, why not toss a hot cup of coffee into the person's face, and then take out the person or run away? The essence of this technique is to use hot liquids to startle, injure and create chaos within the enemy.

煙幕搔乱之法
En Maku Kaku Ran No Ho
(Creating Confusion with a Smoke Curtain Method)

When being pursued the *ninja* would often create fires as he went. The smoke and fire would act as an obstacle for his pursuers. This technique involves setting up such obstacles to create a curtain of smoke or fire. Soldiers actively use this method when retreating. A smoke screen provides a distorted visual covering that allows for movement with less risk of getting hit by snipers. In daily life, a lesson can also be learned from this. Sometimes a smoke screen can be verbal. Create enough fuss and someone's attention is bound to be diverted amidst the confusion.

鬼火之法
Oni Bi No Ho (Fire Spirits Method)

Japanese people were very superstitious about *kami* or "spirits." Unidentified lights at night may have been perceived as ghosts, and so in this technique the use of light to frighten others is used. *Ninjas* used the superstitions of the people to their advantage. In many ways people's superstitions are to some degree culturally dependent. Here's a case to prove my point. I once heard a ghost story in which a few persons saw an apparition appear on a television screen in full color. According to the account the TV was being carried by movers at the time. If that puts chills up your spine, then you could be taken in by this deceptive method.

In today's world there are lines people won't cross because of their religion or other belief system. These things can be used to the ninja's advantage. Psychological warfare is based on this principle. Often times a captured soldier is trained not to fear death. To some there are worse things than death. For instance, a strong belief in one's religion may make one follow religious laws that if violated may mean eternal damnation according to the believer. If such a soldier is kept alive, more information can possibly be retrieved. Play on the other captured person's worst fears and the person can be used to one's advantage.

息討器之法
Soku Toki No Ho (Smoke Blower Method)

Imagine someone walking up to you and lifting a strange object to his mouth and the last thing you see before you are cut down is burning smoke and embers hitting your face. The *ninja* possessed such a device. It was called the *Soku Toki* which strangely translates as "beg to stop device." As the situation suggests it was used by surprise to create confusion and pain long enough to take a person out. In today's times we don't carry around smoldering boxes filled with metsubushi. We could however carry around a cigar and do pretty much the same thing.

About the Author

James Clum is a teacher, writer and artist living in Southern California. He started his martial arts training at the age of 13 in 1980. Dr. Clum is a licensed Doctor of Chiropractor. He holds blackbelts in several martial arts including *Jujitsu*, *Hapkido* and *Aikido*. He has combined the most useful elements of these arts to create Aiki Goshin Ho. This is a type of Aikijutsu which focus on practical self-defense. Dr. Clum is also a Shidoshi or licensed teacher within the Bujinkan organization that teaches *Budo Taijutsu*. Dr. Clum can be reached through his email at jamesnmichelle8@verizon.net

www.azusabujinkan.com

Glossary

Age-rising
Aitekata-opponent, adversary
Amado-striking point at the side of the neck
Aruki- to walk
Ashi-foot
Atama-head
Atemi-striking the body
Budo-martial arts
Bujin-spirits of war
Bujinkan-spirits of war organization
Butsumetsu-striking point at the underarm
Chi-earth
Chi-blood
Chiburi-flicking the blood of a sword
Chudan-middle level
Daijodan-posture with sword held above the head
Daito-long sword
Dan-level
Dogi-training uniform
Dojo-training facility
Doko-angry tiger
Domo arigato gazaimasu-thank you very much
Dori-to seize or capture
Dozo-please go ahead
Fu-wind
Fudo-immoveable
Fudoza-seated posture
Gakure-hidden
Ganseki-big rock
Gassho-hands together
Gedan-lower level
Giri-to cut
Giso-camouflage
Godai-five elements
Goho-five methods
Gyaku-opposite, a joint lock
Hachimonji-shaped like the character for 8

NINJUTSU: ENDURING LEGACY

Hakama-large pleated pants worn by samurai
Hajime-begin
Happa-eight leaves, open hand
Happo-eight directions, eight methods
Henka-variations
Hicho-flying bird
Hidari-left
Hiden-secret transmission
Hikari-light
Hira-flat
Hiza-knee
Ho-method
Hon-foundation
Hodoki-freeing something
Hoko-to embrace
Hokojutsu-ways of walking
Hoshi-star, striking point at inner elbow
Iai maai-correct distance for drawing a sword
Ichi-one
Ichimonji-number one, straight
In Yo-Yin and Yang
Iri-entering
Itami-pain
Jika Tabi-outdoor split toe shoes
Ju-ten
Jumonji-crossed
Judan-upper lever
Junan Taiso-warming up exercises
Jutsu-art
Ka-fire
Kaeshi/Gaeshi-to reverse
Kaiten-to roll, rolling
Kamae-posture
Kami-spirit
Kasane-heavy
Kasumi-mist, striking points at temples
Kata/Gata-form
Kata-single
Kata-shoulder
Katana-sword
Kaze-wind
Keiko-practice
Ken-fist
Ken-sword
Keri/Geri-to kick, a kick
Kihon-basics
Kikaku-demon horns
Kiri-to cut

Kirioroshi-a downward cut with sword
Kiten-flips
Ko-child
Kodama-tree spirits
Koho-to the rear
Koppo-bone breaking, knack
Koroshi-to kill
Koshi-hips
Kosshijutsu-old martial arts using finger attacks
Kote
Ku-emptiness
Kubi-neck
Kudaki-to crush
Kuden-oral transmission
Kumo-cloud
Kuruma-wheel, car
Kuten-arial flips
Kyahan-leg wrappings
Kyoshi-teacher
Kyu-grade
Maai-distance
Maki-to wrap
Metsubushi-blinding powder
Migi-right
Mikkyo-secret teaching of esoteric Buddhism
Mizu-water
Mizu gumo-water spider floatation device
Moguri-earthworm
Mokuso-meditation
Mono-person
Mune-chest
Musha-warrior
Mute-without using the hands
Nage-to throw, a throw
Nagare-flow, to flow
Nagare-striking point on top of forearm near elbow
Nagashi-to flow
Nage-to throw
Naka-middle, center
Nami-wave
Nin-to endure, to bear, stealth
Netto-hot soup
Ni-two
Nihon-Japan
Nihongo-Japanese language
Ninja- a stealthy person
Ninja to-ninja sword
Ninpo-ninja methods

No-of
Noda-shi-home city of Masaaki Hatsumi
Notto-returning the sword to its scabbard
Nuki-to throw
Obi-belt
Omote-outer surface
Onegaishimasu-if you please
Oni-demon
Ori-to break
Oten-cartwheels
Otenki-weather
Otoshi-to drop
Oya-parent
Oyogi-swimming, to swim
Ran-confusion
Rei-respect
Reiho-ettiquette
Ryote-both hands
Ryu-lineage
Ryusui Iki-falling like flowing water
Sabaki-footwork
Samurai-a retainer
Sanpo-three methods
Saya-sword case
Sayu-left and right
Saru-monkey
Seiza-sitting on the instep
Senban-flat plate throwing blades
Sensei-teacher
Shako-mantis shrimp
Shi-finger
Shidoshi-teacher of the warrior ways
Shihan-master teacher
Shiho-four directions
Shin-heart
Shinobi-stealth
Shizen-natural
Shodan-first degree blackbelt
Shomen-shrine at dojo front
Shoto-short sword
Shugendo-type of esoteric Buddhism
Shugyo-training
Shuki-elbow
Shuko-hand claws
Shuriken-throwing blade
Soke-inheritor
Sokki-knee
Soku-foot

Sokuho-to the side
Soto-outside
Sui-water
Suigetsu-water moon (name of striking point at solar plexus
Sutemi-sacrific
Suwari-seated
Suzu-bell, testicles
Tabi-split toe socks
Tachi-sword
Tai-body
Taijutsu-old term referring to unarmed combat
Taiso-physical exercise
Take-bamboo
Tanso-to run away
Teki-enemy
Tekubi-wrist
Tenchi-heaven and earth
Tenkan-turning around
Tengu-goblin
Teppo-gun
Tobi-to fly or leap
Tomoe-comma
Tori-person being attacked in practice
Torite-seizing the hands
Tsuka-sword handle
Tsuba-sword hand guard
Tsuki-a punch
Tsuki-to thrust
Uchi-a strike
Uchi-inner
Ude-arm
Uke-training attacker
Uke-to block, a block
Ukemi-receiving an attack, falling
Ura-inner surface
Ushiro-behind
Uzura-quail
Yamabushi-Shugendo priest, mountain ascetic
Yame-stop
Yari-spear
Yoko-side
Yubi-finger
Waza-techniques
Zanshin-mindfullness
Zenpo-forward
Zori-straw sandals

Bibliography

Hatsumi, Masaaki. *The Way of the Ninja*. 1st. 1. Tokyo, Japan: Kodansha International, 2004. Print.

Hatsumi, Masaaki. *Ninjutsu: History and Tradition*. 1st. Burbank, CA: Unique Publications, 1981. Print.

Hatsumi, Masaaki. *The Essence of Ninjutsu*. 8th. Chicago, Illinois: Contemporary Books, 1988. Print.

Van Donk, Richard. *Shodan no Maki*. 1997. 1. Middletown, California: Bushindo University, 1997. Print.

Van Donk, Richard. *Nidan Manual*. 1994. 2. Middletown, California: Bushindo University, 2006. Print.

Turnball, Stephen. *Ninja AD1460-1650*. 1st. Oxford: Osprey Publishing, 2003. Print.

Ron, Roy. "Shoninki." *Historical Records*. 2009. Ninpo.org, Web. 18 Jan 2010. <http://www.ninpo.org/historicalrecords/shnnkmkrk.htm>.

Printed in Great Britain
by Amazon